CHANGE THE WAY YOU LEAD CHANGE

CHANGE THE WAY YOU LEAD CHANGE

*Leadership Strategies
That REALLY Work*

DAVID M. HEROLD
and
DONALD B. FEDOR

STANFORD BUSINESS BOOKS
An Imprint of Stanford University Press
Stanford, California

Stanford University Press
Stanford, California

Printed in the United States of America on acid-free, archival-quality paper

Library of Congress Cataloging-in-Publication Data

Herold, David M.
    Change the way you lead change : leadership strategies that really work /
David M. Herold and Donald B. Fedor.
        p. cm.
    Includes bibliographical references and index.
    ISBN 978-0-8047-5875-8 (cloth : alk. paper)
    ISBN 978-0-8047-7179-5 (pbk. : alk. paper)
    1. Organizational change. 2. Leadership. I. Fedor, Donald B. II. Title.
    HD58.8.H485 2008
    658.4'092—dc22   2008001986

Typeset by Classic Typography in 10.5/15 Minion

Special discounts for bulk quantities of Stanford Business Books are available
to corporations, professional associations, and other organizations. For details
and discount information, contact the special sales department of Stanford
University Press. Tel: (650) 736-1783, Fax: (650) 736-1784

To Ellie, with love

To my parents, Dorothy and Walter Fedor

CONTENTS

PREFACE

Why another book on organizational change?

You've heard it over and over again. Change is everywhere! Change or perish! The world is changing! Business is changing at the speed of light! Change is the only constant! If you go to Amazon.com and type in "organizational change" you will find, as of this writing, 24,386 entries! If change is so pervasive, and so many have had so much to say about it, you would think that everyone would have unlocked its secrets and figured out how to deal with it.

Unfortunately, when it comes to organizational change initiatives, study after study, conducted by academics, consulting firms, trade associations, or professional magazines, finds that the vast majority of changes, be they restructurings, technology implementations, or business process changes, fail outright or fall far short of expectations. By most estimates, really successful organizational changes occur less than 20 percent of the time. So, we fail, find someone or something to blame, and start all over again.

This state of affairs does not result from a lack of well-accepted prescriptions about how change should be handled. If you want to succeed in change, you are told, you ought to do the following: have and articulate a vision, communicate effectively, inspire people, involve people in decisions about the change, role model the new behaviors, remove obstacles to the change, and reinforce the new behaviors; and, by the way, it would really help if you were also a transformational or charismatic leader.

It's not that people are unaware of these recommendations; they are broadcast, in one way or another, by many books, articles, seminars, and consulting firms. In fact, most of the best-selling books on change provide such prescriptions for implementing whatever change one has in mind. Unfortunately, while such approaches provide an often-yearned-for level of simplicity (for example, "follow these six steps to effective change"), they simply don't deliver the results. As Louis Lavelle, a book reviewer for *BusinessWeek* magazine, so aptly put it: "To hear most authors of business books tell it, there is no management conundrum so great that it can't be solved by the deft application of seven or eight basic principles. The authors are almost always wrong: Big public companies have too many moving parts to conform to any set of simple precepts."[1]

In our own executive teaching and consulting, we increasingly suspected that these "conventional wisdoms" were not enough. People seemed increasingly cynical about change. These change guidelines and prescriptions were too simplistic to address the complexities surrounding change in most organizations, they were viewed as niceties or luxuries not heeded by many organizations, or they were seen as idealistic or impractical given the situations most people found themselves in. What's worse, often, even when these guidelines were followed, results were still not satisfactory.

So we started asking executives to think of a change that didn't go as well as they would have liked, and to identify the key factor that may have been responsible. We found out that many of the root causes of failure were not related to faulty change process. Rather, they were often systemic or situational factors that doomed the planned changes no matter how much attention was paid to process. For example, changes that don't make sense, suffer from lack of leadership, or push people beyond their capabilities will not succeed no matter what methods are used to implement them. Yet even as we struggled to incorporate these many complicating factors into our own thinking, more and more books were coming out taking the opposite view. Namely, they minimized or even trivialized the important issues and glossed over management's critical role in leading change. For example, the wildly popular book *Who Moved My Cheese?* suggests that the fault lies with the broad base of organizational members who are just not comfortable enough or nimble enough to get with change programs. We all just need to learn to love and embrace change and everything will be okay.

We also noticed that while some disappointing change efforts could be diagnosed as suffering from "communication," "vision," or "sense of urgency" issues, more often than not, the lists of most recommended change steps did not map onto leaders' lists of root causes for failed changes. These recommendations could not explain failures due to pursuit of bad change ideas; failures due to the inadequacy of those asked to lead change; failures attributable to the behaviors of those expected to implement the change; failures attributable to cultural and other, intraorganizational factors; or failures attributable to factors in the organization's environment.

We found that almost all advice about organizational change focuses on a few steps applied to a single change. Yet we found few people who live in a "one change at a time" environment; they live on a roller coaster of change. Many times the different and overlapping changes are driven by different events, are led by different executives, and originate from different parts of the organization using different consultants. Organizations rarely have the luxury of shutting everything else out while they concentrate on a given change initiative.

Slowly, we came to understand that successful changes require leaders to develop better ways of analyzing (1) *what* they think they want or need to change, (2) what they know about *themselves* and the *others* who will be asked to lead and make the behavioral adjustments implied by the change, and (3) what they know about the *context* in which the change is to occur, especially about what other changes are taking place. Only then can change leaders develop a strategy for *how* they will go about it, when they will do what, and how fast they can move.

The savvy change leader understands the complex interplay of these issues. When Lou Gerstner assumed the helm at IBM, he "shocked" the business press and Wall Street analysts when he stated, "The last thing IBM needs now is a vision." We can be reasonably sure he had some vision in mind, or he would not have taken the job. Yet he understood that as an outsider, it would have been a mistake to march in and proclaim he knew exactly what was wrong and what new directions the organization should go in. He needed to fix some things that were obviously broken (not requiring a vision), he needed to size up who he had to work with, he had to gain credibility with his followers, and he had to understand the environment (internal and external). Ultimately, he had the opportunity to enact his vision, but the "what" and "how" he chose were shaped by the "who" and the "context" as he saw them. What seemed like an inauspicious beginning turned out to be an incredibly successful organizational transformation.

Contrast this with other outsiders who march in proclaiming the wisdom of their vision and bull-headedly push forth, with little regard for the organization's culture or history, the opinions of various thought leaders, and without really understanding the situation (possible examples—Carly Fiorina at Hewlett-Packard and Bob Nardelli at Home Depot). These leaders usually meet with disastrous personal and organizational results. Thus it is not whether one does or does not need a vision for major changes. Rather, the role played by a grand vision is dependent on who the leader is and what situation he or she finds him- or herself in (as well as other qualifiers we'll discuss later on), which will determine what the first step of the change process should be and how it should unfold.

Realizing that change success or failure is better understood in terms of the interplay of several important factors, we set out to identify and explore these factors. To supplement our understanding of the many writings in this area, we embarked on a series of studies, spanning ten years, that examined more than three hundred changes and over eight thousand individuals who have lived through them. We then reality-tested and shaped these learnings by bouncing them off hundreds of managers we encountered in executive education and consulting settings.

We also looked for insights from popular press descriptions of organizational changes and change leaders. Did events in the "real world" support the general principles and frameworks we were developing? Thus our observations span the gamut from academic studies, attending to the rigor and methods of scientific inquiry, to organizational cases and anecdotes reported in the media, to the experiences of people in the know—those living change on a day-to-day basis.

Given our journey, and the tremendous respect we've developed for the complexity and nuances of the topic, we do not intend this book to be "the total answer" (if there is ever such a thing). If nothing else, we've figured out that change is never a straightforward, stepwise, linear, or easily prescribed process. Rather, it is messy and complicated, and its outcomes are easily swayed by a host of factors, making prediction of success difficult at best. So what is your choice? You can throw your hands up and say, "This is too difficult or complex," and thus relegate the problem to the simple prescriptions that already exist, to intuition, or to the realm of art. Or you can try to tackle the problem head on and become more fully aware of what needs to be considered when faced with a significant organizational change. The bottom line is that successful organizational change is really hard work. With all due respect to another popular book on the subject, change is definitely not for dummies!

To use a baseball analogy, lifetime .300 hitters get inducted into the Baseball Hall of Fame. The evidence seems to suggest that .300 would also be a pretty good change batting average in most organizations. Well, you might say, three out of ten isn't so hot. It is if you consider how difficult the task is, and that most people do worse! This book is designed to help you improve your change success batting average, not to make it 1.000!

WHAT DO WE MEAN BY CHANGE?

At this point, we need to say something about what we mean by *organizational change* and how we will use the term. We use the term *change* or *organizational change* to mean demands placed on organizations or organizational subunits that require significant departures from people's current routines and behaviors, *and the success of which depends upon the support of those affected.*

As such, whether the change represents a total strategic transformation of a business; a major restructuring; or the implementation of a new technology, business system, or process is not really important for our purposes. Nor is it important for our purposes that a change affect the whole organization. When we use the term *change,* we mean something initiated by one or more organizational leaders, intended to achieve certain results through the modification of other people's behaviors or routines, with the success or failure to achieve these modifications having consequences for the particular organizational unit or the organization as a whole.

WHO IS THIS BOOK FOR?

In this book, we hope to stimulate thinking about change among several important audiences. We hope to convince executives that change leadership does not lend itself to quick-reading, parable-laden, simplistic prescriptions. Change is a serious matter, and the landscape is strewn with organizations and leaders that have failed to understand it.

In a survey of 1,087 corporate directors, reported in *BusinessWeek,* it was found that 31 percent of CEOs fired by their boards were removed because they mismanaged change, more than any other single reason given.[2] Who knows how many managers below the CEO level have met the same fate. Change leadership is increasingly considered an important competency for advancement in organizations, as well as for being selected to key positions. Though Bob Nardelli was widely seen as the better operating executive at GE, some have speculated that Jack Welch chose Jeff Immelt to succeed him precisely because he was more adept at managing change.[3]

For students, especially those enrolled in business, management, or organizational psychology courses, we hope to convey the notion that change can, and should be, considered from a more scientific and scholarly approach, and that a better grasp of organizational change is an indispensable competency required of any future leader.

Finally, we think consultants also will gain insights from reading this book. We hope such insights will help them better identify potential pitfalls in change programs, improve their ability to place a specific consulting engagement in the larger context of what else is going on in the client organization, and generally help facilitate the changes they've been asked to help design and implement. Such an orientation will serve both the client and the consultant well. Thus, regardless of your interest or perspective, change deserves your serious attention!

ACKNOWLEDGMENTS

We want to thank the many people, too numerous to name, who have shaped our thinking and been supportive of our efforts. This includes our Organizational Behavior colleagues at Georgia Tech, the many students in both our regular and our executive MBA programs who suffered through many versions of these materials, the reviewers who read portions of the manuscript for the publisher, and the editors and reviewers of the journals who published our research and provided encouragement and feedback concerning our approach to the topics of change and change leadership.

We want to especially thank Luis Martins, our colleague at Georgia Tech, Mike Hopp at Lockheed Martin Corp., and Michael Bowen at the University of South Florida for their reviews and comments on earlier versions of the manuscript, and Steven Caldwell and Vicky Liu for their research assistance.

CHANGE THE WAY YOU LEAD CHANGE

THE REALITIES OF CHANGE

"For every complex question there is a simple answer. And it's wrong."
H. L. Mencken

After many months of agonizing investigation, the bipartisan commission studying the September 11 attacks released its findings on July 22, 2004. The commission's consensus was that the United States suffered a major intelligence failure caused, in part, by organizational issues within and between agencies charged with our nation's safety, including the FBI, the Central Intelligence Agency (CIA), the Federal Aviation Authority (FAA), the National Security Council (NSC), and others. The report called for a sweeping set of changes in the management and coordination of the nation's intelligence functions.

Although this event took place several years ago, can one find a more clear and compelling case for organizational change? Can one deny the realities— the pressures for change, the documented performance failures, the tragic consequences of these failures, and the dire prospects if such performance issues are not remedied? All the requisite conditions for successful change prescribed by change books and articles are embodied in this scenario—Envision a different future! Done! Create a sense of urgency! Done! Raise dissatisfaction with the status quo! Done! Generate motivation to change! Done! Separate from the past! Done! From an organizational change perspective, this ought to be a "slam-dunk"—all that's left is to do it!

In reality, most media commentators were quick to note that implementation of the recommendations would be extremely difficult. "Politics and resistance to change make swift action on 9/11 panel's advice unlikely," read a headline in the *New York Times* the morning after the report's release;[1] this despite the fact that the commission noted that future attacks are not only probable, they are almost certain. In fact, a year later, members of the commission, concerned that their recommendations had not been acted on, planned for another, privately financed report to examine the government's response, or lack thereof. Fully five years after the initial shock, in the 2006 elections, implementing the *9/11 Commission Report*'s recommendations was still a campaign issue. Only in the early days of the 2007 Congressional session did the House pass a bill aimed at implementing the Commission's report.

Clearly, urgency is often a necessary, but not sufficient, condition for ensuring successful organizational change. Many companies across a wide variety of industries, such as AT&T, HP, Xerox, GM, and Ford, have experienced and correctly perceived the pressures to change; that is, the urgency was there. Yet experience, as well as reviews by prominent academics and consultants, leads us to conclude that between 67 percent and 80 percent of change efforts, large and small, fail. McKinsey consultants, studying change initiatives in forty different companies, concluded that 58 percent failed to meet the value originally proposed in the business case for the change, with 20 percent capturing less than a third of the value they had expected.[2]

CEOs Durk Jager at P&G, Jacques Nasser at Ford, Richard Thoman at Xerox, Philip Purcell at Morgan Stanley, Robert Nardelli at Home Depot, and Carly Fiorina at Hewlett-Packard departed, or were removed, not because they failed to see the need for change in their organizations, nor because they didn't try to drive change. They failed because their changes either did not yield the expected results, or because the toll these changes took upon their organizations was deemed to exceed the benefits.

This illustrates several very important issues. First, although *the need to change* is often quite clear, *what* needs changing is often much less so, and *how* to create meaningful and lasting change is a totally different and more difficult matter. Just because a compelling case can be made for change doesn't mean the particular change is worth doing, that it will be embraced, or that it will be successful. Second, although "change or perish" is a catchy phrase, the reality is that many of today's struggling organizations have not been at all timid about initiating change. If anything, frequent and often gut-wrenching changes, along with their attendant impact on individuals and even communities, have been organizational realities for the past two decades.

When Jacques Nasser took over at Ford in 1999, he initiated a major restructuring of the entire business, dubbed "Ford 2000." When William Ford took over, after Nasser's ouster, he announced another major restructuring. In early 2006, after disastrous results, the company announced its third makeover in seven years, dubbed "The Way Forward." By the end of that year, Ford had brought in another CEO, from the outside, to see if he could do any better. Throughout this time, it was clear to everyone the business had to change in some fundamental ways if it was to survive.

It's the *nature of the response* to this realization that is the important issue, and the one many organizations, like Ford, have had a difficult time mastering. Although many organizations have undergone repeated and painful changes, their fortunes have often still declined. Many changed but perished anyway, or had near-death experiences. The imperative of change is one thing, the chosen response is another, the emotions and realities as the change unfolds are still another, and the relationship between organizational changes and organizational success is something else again.

Clearly, our penchant for the "quick fix" (for example, the five steps or seven steps to successful change) just hasn't served us well. If anything, it has led to one failure after another and has left many in our organizations confused, anxious, cynical, and often feeling angry and burnt-out. Creating significant change in organizations is a daunting, complex, and somewhat unpredictable business—far too complicated to let simple prescriptions be one's guide, appealing though they may be. Organizations have to come to grips with the fact that so many of their attempts at change fail to realize their intended goals. As we noted earlier, all the evidence seems to suggest that people are not very good at this game of change—their approaches to change seem broken, and they need to fix them!

THE CASE FOR CHANGE

There is no question that all organizations, not just business, need to adapt in order to survive. Adaptation implies change, but change does not necessarily imply adaptation. That is, to adapt you need to change, but not just any change will get you there. This turns out to be an important issue, and one that is often overlooked when the only explanation usually heard for a change is that "we must change to survive." True, but it must be an *adaptive* change, not just any change!

The pressures for change in today's world are formidable. The competitive landscape is constantly changing as business models, economic conditions, labor markets, geopolitical forces, demographics, and consumer preferences keep shifting. Technological changes affect how we do business, how we manage, and how we drive major changes in whole industries. For some organizations, it isn't just these forces that are the source of pressures to change, but also their volatility. Fluctuations in these forces create uncertainties that require their own adaptive responses if organizations are to cope with them. As *Forbes* magazine recently noted, "The pace of change is accelerating. . . . Globalization is not the problem. Change—that's our challenge."[3]

Another major driver of organizational change is feedback about performance. Negative feedback about outcomes spurs organizations to take corrective actions. Although economic issues, such as drops in revenue or profit, or loss of market share, are the obvious feedback mechanisms, noneconomic issues, such as loss of talent, low morale, ethical lapses, environmental impact, or community relations, may also signal a need to consider significant change.

Although the forces just mentioned represent environmental signals that put organizations on notice that they may need to change, two other drivers of change not necessarily related to such signaling also need to be considered. First, senior leadership may have (or new leadership may bring) a change in philosophy, or a belief in practices, processes, or programs that may or may not be in direct response to environmental pressures, but which they believe will improve the business. Such initiatives create significant organizational changes. For example, many an executive has decreed that his or her organization adopt Six Sigma, BPR (Business Process Reengineering), ERP (Enterprise Resource Planning), lean manufacturing, or new employee evaluation and compensation systems. These initiatives precipitate a host of changes throughout the organization, many of these being quite traumatic, with their effects long-lasting.

A second source of changes not clearly signaled by changes in one's environment may simply be senior executives' desire to leave their imprint on the organization or to demonstrate to others they are changing the status quo and, therefore, are being proactive in their leadership role. As more leadership transitions occur, either because the environment has not been kind to the organization or because leaders have not shown themselves to be up to the job, this need to "leave one's mark" simply generates more and more change.

Clearly there are more than enough drivers of change in today's business environment. In a recent survey of more than 750 of the world's top CEOs, conducted by IBM, 65 percent said they plan to radically change their organizations in the next two years. Astoundingly, however, 80 percent admit their organizations have not been successful at managing change in the past.[4]

The problem does not seem to be management's reluctance or inability to conjure up changes. Rather, the problem seems to be an inability to successfully implement such changes, and the fact that proposed changes so often exceed organizations' capacity to digest them! Thus the real question is not whether change is good or bad or whether it is needed or not. It is whether leaders can balance the need to drive change and their organization's capacity to change effectively. They need to carefully consider their situation and choose a change path they think will be appropriate in the long run, rather than engage in knee-jerk, copycat, or faddish change trends.

"CHANGE OR PERISH" VERSUS "CHANGE AND PERISH"

At a management development seminar facilitated by one of the authors, a manager from a major telecommunications company recounted how a consultant had been hired by her company to address managers about the "management of change." The purpose of the presentation was to assure managers that change is an inevitable and healthy organizational reality. The consultant was essentially trying to reenergize the organization's middle managers in an atmosphere that had become rather bleak as change upon change, usually resulting in personal hardships, swept over the company. The basic premise of the presentation was that changes in the business environment are causing, and will continue to cause, ever-more rapid changes in our organizations and our lives.

The managers were warned that this reality of increasing frequency of changes meant they will have to learn to practice "no recovery management," which the consultant defined as not having the luxury of time to adapt to changes. Rather, managers have to get used to adapting to change more or less instantaneously, because the next change will be upon them soon.

Thousands of such presentations have probably been made to corporate audiences everywhere. The graphic that often accompanies these "insights" about change is the ubiquitous sine curve, borrowed from engineering, showing the increasing frequency and amplitude of change "waves," thereby "proving" the forces for change are becoming more severe and more frequent, with the time between waves getting shorter and shorter. Although appealing, this notion of constant organizational turmoil being necessitated by ever-more rapid environmental pressures, if accepted on faith, has several dangerous implications for the management of organizations.

First, although it appeals to a Darwinian view that only the fittest will survive, it confuses mere change with successful adaptation. Using this argument for creating an environment of continuous change raises the question of whether the changes will, in fact, help the organization in its long-term efforts to master its environment. Confusing the frequency and severity of change with successful adaptation would lead us to conclude that struggling companies such as Sears, Kodak, GM, and Ford are some of the most successful companies around.

Second, not only does constant upheaval not help organizations succeed, we must accept the fact that organizational members suffer real costs from the instability, anxiety, stress, and dislocation caused by the constant turmoil of change initiatives piled on top of change initiatives. Peter Brabeck, CEO of Nestlé, the giant Swiss food company, put it this way in an interview in the *Harvard Business Review:* "You cannot underestimate the traumatic impact of abrupt change, the distraction it causes in running the business, the fear it provokes in people, the demands it makes on management's time."[5]

This view is consistent with the vast amounts of social science evidence concerning how individuals and, by implication, organizations respond to constant adaptation pressures in the face of finite, inadequate, or even diminishing coping resources. The physical, psychological, and emotional toll on people undergoing change is very real. Assuming we can extract *favorable* change responses from our organizational members over and over again is a recipe for failure.

Conversely, treating response capacities as scarce commodities, and doing everything to conserve them, may ensure they are available for future deployment for other, really necessary changes. Organizations can only change as fast as the people within them are able and willing to embrace change!

A third danger in too readily chanting the "change or perish" mantra is that such explanations are often used as a means of absolving leaders of the responsibility for actually managing change. Is it possible senior leadership has *created* some of the conditions that now require radical changes to correct? Leaders don't just report the unpleasant news—they often make the news. Not fully recognizing the role leadership plays in organizational change leads to the legitimization of practices, programs, management fads, and constant turmoil in the name of "the sky is falling," while at the same time eroding organizational and personal resources as organizations become overwhelmed with change, resources that will be essential when really important changes become necessary.

Finally, blaming everything on "changes out there" and leadership's failure to take personal responsibility for the nature, frequency, and severity of changes has the tendency to shift the blame for failed changes to those charged with implementing them. Thus people are labeled as "resisters," middle managers are labeled as "blockers," and the problem is framed in terms of the inadequacies of lower-level organizational participants. If only people would be more welcoming of change, facile in their adaptation, less focused on their own needs, and just more committed to the organization and its goals, change leadership would be easy. What if those "resisting" have a good reason for doing so? What if they have insights the change planners do not have? What if the change really is a dumb idea? What if there are reasons why it just won't work?

When Julie Roehm, an advertising whiz kid, was hired by Wal-Mart from the automobile industry to be senior vice president for marketing and to breathe fresh life into their advertising and marketing, she moved swiftly to challenge the culture (and the existing executives) with edgy campaigns and new pushes into fashion and home decorating. She also dumped their old advertising agency and hired a new one. When she was ousted *after only eleven months* on the job she noted, "Anytime there's someone new or who represents change, you always get a feeling that's not always welcoming. . . . My visibility created a general amount of animosity."[6]

Such observations by leaders trying to create change but who run into difficulties or fall flat on their faces speak to a lack of introspection or awareness about one's role as an agent of change. What role did you play in creating the animosity? What about the miscalculations about what you can change and how fast? What about getting people on your side before barreling forth with radical changes? What about strategizing about how to maximize your effectiveness? What about taking stock of how the new setting differs from the one in which you previously succeeded? What about first trying to understand the setting and the people so that you know what you have to work with?

Some leaders use this patronizing "blame the victim" mentality to deflect attention from their own failures in handling change. They use it to shift the discussion from the merits of the change and how it was handled and toward the inadequacy of the change targets. Such an orientation has spawned endless books, seminars, and training programs aimed at getting "them" to embrace change—all enthusiastically supported and paid for by the change instigators. We've seen the enemy, and it is "them."

Although there is no question that environmental pressures have created adaptation demands on most organizations, not just those in the business world, leaders need to be careful they don't assume that all changes are adaptive, and even when changes are adaptive, leaders need to consider how many such changes, and how fast, the organization can digest. Speaking to business students at Texas A&M University, Robert Nardelli, then CEO of Home Depot, was quoted as saying, "The rate of change internally has to be greater than the rate of change externally or else you're pedaling backward."[7] There is nothing in this prescription that precludes us from pedaling furiously, but in circles, or off the nearest cliff!

THE COST OF CHANGE

Everyone seems to agree change is essential for survival, and constant change seems inevitable if one accepts that the environment is constantly changing. Unfortunately, most organizations have not enjoyed a great deal of success when implementing change for the purpose of better aligning with their environments. Certainly, there are cases in which organizations have done a masterful job of reading the environmental challenge, developing a change plan, and implementing that plan successfully. Successful transitions and transformations do occur. Witness the ability of Anne Mulcahy to take an extremely difficult situation at Xerox and seemingly be able to "right the boat" and steer a new course; witness A. G. Lafley taking over P&G after a tumultuous period in which his predecessor, Durk Jager, tried and failed to introduce radical changes. Lafley has succeeded in taking the company to a new level.

Unfortunately, these represent the exceptions more than the rule. The cost of frequent and significant change for many organizations and all their stakeholders has been tremendous. Worse, even after incurring such costs, many organizations faltered or failed anyway, or the costs greatly exceeded the benefits of the change. The cost of change can be broken down into three broad, but not totally independent, categories of consequences:

- Personal costs
- Changes in organizational capabilities
- Economic impact

Personal costs of change represent the toll changes take on the personal and professional lives of those undergoing the change, as well as those initiating it. These would include changes in the quality of life, work-life balances, stress, and career consequences such as job changes, disruptions, or income changes. From our everyday experiences, we know that having to be available 24/7; working increasingly longer hours; being separated from family; losing leisure time; and experiencing the stress associated with fear, uncertainty, loss of security, and instability are the price we so often associate with organizational pressures and turmoil. Earlier we noted that mismanaging change was the most frequent reason corporate directors give for firing CEOs. Although we don't have data on those below the CEO level, our experience suggests that many a manager has suffered career derailments for either mismanaging change or being associated with ill-conceived or mismanaged changes. This is true even when the manager simply inherited the change, ending up as a scapegoat.

The *capabilities* of an organization are the resources that make up the intangible assets of the organization, which include a company's reputation, its human assets, its brands, its culture, its technology, and its inventiveness. Significant organizational changes can enhance or degrade such capabilities. For example, changes that drive away talented people will damage the organization's capabilities in the area of human capital. Changes that erode the public's confidence in an organization's service orientation, technical capabilities, or ethical conduct will similarly represent costs associated with the degradation of these capabilities. It's an uphill battle to gain back lost customers or restock lost corporate talent, memory, or intelligence.

However, both personal costs and the destruction of organizational capabilities have been largely ignored in the discussion of organizational change. This is primarily because the arguments for change are often framed in terms of *economic imperatives.* In such arguments, personal costs and organizational capability losses are treated as if they really aren't costs at all just because we can't immediately put a price tag on them. Let's face it, if the economic justification for change is there (at least in theory), not much is made of the pain along the way. That is, until such costs become all too evident and their economic impact cannot be ignored. For instance, turnover among key talent will eventually be noticed, and remedies sought. Low ratings in customer satisfaction surveys will eventually be noticed, especially if accompanied by declining sales, and steps will be taken (for example, the rehiring of people previously laid off) to ameliorate the situation.

Thus, although the human and organizational tolls associated with frequent and severe changes are real, though sometimes difficult to quantify, promoters of constant change often justify such costs on the basis of responsibilities to shareholders and short-term Wall Street expectations. Given our economic system, if organizational vitality, growth, and economic viability improve as a function of a change, or a series of changes, few would challenge the price paid. The ends seem to justify the means. However, we've already provided some suggestions that, if anything, very often investors and other stakeholders are also poorly served by such turmoil.

We are not aware of a single study that looks at either a broad range of organizations or focuses on a particular type of change (such as restructurings, mergers, downsizing, business process reengineering) which has concluded, on average, that change yields the expected economic benefits. Yet, clearly, at the individual company level many such changes have indeed been successful in yielding economic benefits. So there must be more to it than just the "what" of change; it must have something to do with how leaders in such organizations conceive, introduce, and implement the change.

If we cannot make blanket statements about the economic benefits of major changes (to the contrary, the blanket statements we can make are largely negative), what about individual companies' track records? Often, major organizational changes are separated in financial statements as "restructuring charges," meaning that they constitute nonrecurring charges, and, as such, should not obscure or seemingly wipe out operating earnings; this seems fair enough. When, however, do such repeated charges become recurring costs, reflecting the failure of change efforts and suggesting constant turmoil as a way of doing business rather than just temporary adaptation costs?

For example, Kodak, in trying to transform itself from a film company to a digital photography company, has gone through more than a decade of gut-wrenching changes during which shareholders, managers, employees, vendors, and whole communities have endured a great deal of trauma. Between 1992 and 2006, the company took such "one-time" restructuring charges *every year,* wiping out more than one-half of the more than $12 billion in operating earnings over the same period.

When CEO Antonio Perez was interviewed in the *New York Times,* he was asked what he thinks of Wall Street's pessimism about the prospects for his company. He replied, "We said in 2003 that it would take us four years to transform this company. The first two years were loaded with restructuring costs, and the analysts are reacting to that."[8] What about the restructuring costs between 1992 and 2003? Don't they count? Or does the clock start anew with every change in leadership? Because, as we've seen, mismanaged change often leads to the ouster of CEOs; if the slate is wiped clean with each leadership change, the economic and social tolls of change are therefore obscured. Leaders may be able to dismiss events that preceded their own tenure in the organization, but the employees, the rest of the organization, and various stakeholders cannot.

Kodak is clearly not the only example demonstrating that merely creating lots of change will not necessarily improve one's fortunes. Earlier, we briefly mentioned Ford as an example of the failure of significant and continuous change, even in the face of accurately perceived environmental pressures. When Jacques Nasser took over as CEO in 1999 (following Alex Trotman's efforts to remake the company), he promptly embarked on an extremely ambitious (some might say brutal) series of initiatives intended to make Ford not only a top carmaker but also one of the world's top companies. He overhauled management practices, instituted a new performance ranking system, hired consultants to help him shake up Ford's culture, initiated new quality programs, and went on an acquisition binge.

Unfortunately, Nasser never had a chance to see the transformation through. Within two years, there were calls for his removal, which did take place thirty-four months after his tenure began. In reviewing Nasser's actions, the business press was almost unanimous—too much change, too quickly, accompanied by a leadership style that failed to rally people to support his initiatives. As noted in *BusinessWeek*, "Nasser had stretched himself too thin. . . . He has pushed Ford in a host of ambitious new directions, piling on one initiative after another."[9] Just four months before his removal, Nasser told *BusinessWeek* he rejected the notion that he was driving change too fast. "If there are any regrets," he said, "it's that we're not moving fast enough."[10] Apparently, he was the only one who felt that way.

Lest we need more evidence that simply driving lots of change will not bring us economic nirvana, consider this quote about A. G. Lafley's replacement of Durk Jager as CEO of Procter & Gamble: "Jager had charged into office determined to rip apart P&G's insular culture and remake it from the bottom up. Instead of pushing P&G to excel, however, the torrent of proclamations and initiatives during Jager's 17-month reign nearly brought the venerable company to a grinding halt."[11]

It is important to remember that not all organizational changes meet the same fate as the ones we've illustrated. Our point is that these were (are) all successful companies, icons of American business, staffed by talented people, able to attract the best and the brightest, having great staffs and able to hire the finest consultants. Yet successful change has often eluded them. Given the many studies showing serious problems with returns from major change efforts, and these specific examples of company misadventures that resulted in major economic and personal losses, we have to conclude that the economic justification for the "change or perish" mentality is not quite evident.

CONCLUSION

The pressures for change are real, but they cannot, and should not, be used as an excuse for careening from one change to another, no matter how sound the new direction seems to be in the abstract. We do not live in the abstract. Adaptation to new realities requires change, but not all change will get you there. What to change, how to change it, when to change it, and at what cost are all critically important considerations.

Globalization, new technologies, market shifts, and greater competition are very real. However, it is leaders who need to develop the strategy, plan the changes, implement them, track them, assess their consequences, and align everything to ensure that these forces for change are addressed. Leaders are responsible for assessing environmental conditions, assessing organizational realities and capabilities, and carefully choosing a change path and an implementation process that is likely to be adaptive rather than just disruptive and painful.

The challenge for leaders is to understand that change consumes scarce psychological as well as economic resources. Therefore, it should be carefully planned and even more carefully implemented so as to get the maximum "bang for the buck" in terms of improved adaptation to environmental exigencies. To simply squander adaptation resources (organizational or personal) on one change after another is a recipe for disaster.

In this book, we assume that organizational leaders are in the best position to sense the environmental pressures operating on the company. Kodak saw the need to transform itself into a digital company; Hewlett-Packard and IBM realized the need to become players in computer services, rather than just in hardware; the domestic automobile companies understand what's happening to them; the U.S. government is well aware of the threat of terrorism.

The issue is not so much whether senior leadership sees the need for change. It is whether what they do subsequent to this realization results in an appropriate response. The problem does not seem to be complacency in the face of change. By and large, most organizational failures do not result from a misguided sense that the business environment is benign, or from a dearth of ideas about change. Instead, failure emanates from the *choices* of *what* to change, *how* to change it, *when* to change it, *how to deal with the anticipated and unanticipated consequences* of driving the particular change, and how to manage the variety of *simultaneous* or overlapping changes that major transformations invariably require or that organizations typically confront. That is the role of change leadership!

2

REFRAMING THE CHANGE DILEMMA

"Insanity: doing the same thing over and over again and expecting different results."
Albert Einstein

When it comes to managing change in organizations, why do people tend to do the same things over and over again even though the results are so often unsatisfactory? Why do they have such a difficult time with change? We have found that some of the reasons have to do with certain "blind spots," assumptions, and preconceptions many people have about how to go about change. For example:

- Jumping too quickly from a business imperative to a particular "solution," not adequately exploring alternatives

- Failing to acknowledge personal biases, values, and agendas in formulating change "solutions"

- Being more focused on *what* to change and *how fast* than on planning how to make it work

- Underestimating the costs and challenges associated with change (especially the human component), while overestimating the benefits

- Failing to assess the environment's capacity to sustain the change

- Becoming impatient with changes already started and quickly moving on to the next business issue

- Confusing the authority to make changes with the leadership necessary to successfully implement them

Contributing to these barriers to successfully framing the change dilemma is the fact that most treatments of change, be they books, articles, case studies, popular press articles, or management development seminars, also largely ignore these issues and only try to answer the question "HOW do you introduce, manage, and/or institutionalize change?" Thus it is not surprising that most of what we read or hear has to do with what is called the change *process;* that is, the importance of having a change vision, how to communicate that vision, how to get people's support, how to treat people during change, how to motivate through reinforcement or celebration, and how to make change "stick."

Imagine going down to your local home improvement store and standing in front of the do-it-yourself book section. Someone asks, "Can I help you find something?" You answer, "Yes, I want a book about building." After the initial look of amazement or amusement wears off, the person trying to help you is likely to try to pin you down a bit more, perhaps asking, "*What* is it you're trying to build?" Ah, you think to yourself, does it matter? Well, silly me! "As a matter of fact," you answer, "I want to build a patio just like the one in this picture, with multiple levels, built-in seating, a barbeque pit, fountains, and recessed lighting."

"Have you ever done masonry work?" asks the clerk. "Well, no." "Have you ever done plumbing or electrical work?" "No." "Who will be doing this work?" "Just me and my two teenagers; oh, and I forgot to mention, I only have my one-week vacation to work on this project, and there is only eight feet of level ground behind my kitchen where I plan to build it." After a few moments of reflection, the store clerk reaches for a book titled *Building a Simple Deck in Two Weekends,* hands it to you, and says, "Why don't you look through this and consider whether this might not be a better idea." You take the clerk's advice, buy the book, read it, and return to the store to buy the materials; in four days you and your kids build a nice little twelve-by-eight-foot deck off your kitchen, and you enjoy it from that time on.

What's our point? Obviously, the question of "how" doesn't make much sense until you address the question of "what." The integration of a new acquisition will involve different process issues than those for reorganizing a division or introducing new technology. Furthermore, both the "what" and "how" may need to be revisited once we consider the "who," "when," "how fast," and "under what conditions," or context for the change. For example, the leader who has established strong bonds with his or her followers will face a very different change challenge in proposing a reorganization than one who is new to the setting, or has not enjoyed a particularly strong relationship with those affected by the change.

Similarly, introducing certain changes when business is good can be an entirely different matter than introducing the same changes when business is in decline, or when the change is one of many other ongoing changes. Although you may have started off with a broad sense of what the nature of the change should be, these other considerations will often necessitate altering your thinking about what can be accomplished, how fast, and what it will take in terms of "how" to approach the implementation. Most treatments of change totally ignore all of these concerns. As in our home improvement example, how can we think about change process without contemplating the content, context, actors, and other confounding factors?

THE KEY COMPONENTS OF A CHANGE FRAMEWORK

Most organizational change initiatives suffer from some of the shortsightedness evident in our naive deck builder in the example earlier. Namely, a change idea is generated, usually based on some perceived business need, an execution plan is developed that may vary in its thoroughness, and then a "roll out" is announced. This sequence is depicted in Figure 2.1.

The perceived strategic or business imperative and its translation into a change target are intentionally shown with broken lines to denote that this linkage may not always be clear or straightforward even to those initiating the change. Leaders pursuing a particular change do so for a variety of motives— business strategy is but one. Personal beliefs about what works or does not, the desire to emulate another organization, or advice from others may all shape this decision. Consequently, people may often disagree on what changes might best serve a given business strategy. The choice of what to change may also reflect various personal biases, preferences, predispositions, and even deeply rooted needs such as ego, power, or achievement. For some change initiatives the linkage to the business situation is obvious, for some this linkage may be logical but still open to argument or reasonable alternatives, while some such decisions leave us thinking, "Why this change?"

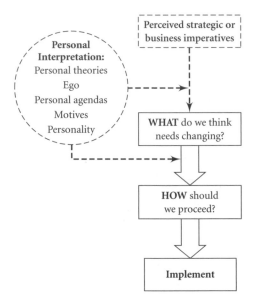

Figure 2.1. Typical sequence of a change project

Similarly, the HOW should we proceed question may be influenced by the same subjectivities as the choice of WHAT. For example, some leaders believe in secrecy in planning the implementation, some are more open and inclusive. Some leaders are more socially aware of the implications of the change, others are not. Some think you get things done by edict, others understand you get things done by persuasion and collaboration. These personal theories will shape the implementation plan, and the launch will follow accordingly.

We often ask executive and managerial audiences to reflect on a particular change that did not go well and identify the single best explanation for what went wrong. The reader may want to do the same. We find changes that did not meet expectations, or that failed outright, typically have done so for one or more of the following reasons:

1. *What was changed failed to address the problem* (for example, cosmetic changes, staffing changes, reorganizations, or new technologies that were not able to deal with the underlying issues or support the overall business strategy).

2. *The change addressed the wrong or even a nonexistent problem* (for example, still another restructuring when the basic strategy is not working).

3. *The person leading the change was not up to the job* (for example, was not trusted, didn't have the support of those involved, was not supportive, lost interest halfway through, lacked critical skills).

4. There was *poor adaptation on the part of those expected to change their behavior* (for example, lack of skills, lack of motivation, stubborn resistance, lack of fit with new requirements, tired of change).

5. *Events or factors inside the organization derailed the change* (for example, incompatibility of compensation system, cultural issues, inadequate processes, other changes taking place simultaneously, lack of time).

6. *Events or factors outside the organization derailed the change* (for example, change in economic conditions, loss of key client or supplier, actions of a competitor, labor market factors).

7. *The process used to implement the change was flawed* (for example, poorly communicated, not sufficiently explained or supported, not sensitive to the needs of those whose support was crucial).

People can generally think of changes that fit all of the preceding descriptions, with most failed initiatives probably suffering from more than one of these shortcomings. If we look at each of these potential causes of failure as a category or set of issues that may derail change efforts, then a framework for thinking about change would need to incorporate all of them. In other words, the complexity we've talked about reflects the need to consider all of these factors. To facilitate our discussion, let's label each of these problem areas:

- Categories 1 and 2 in the previous list represent the WHAT of change, or the content and nature of the change.

- Categories 3 and 4 can be considered issues of WHO; that is, the critical players and how they influence the outcomes of change efforts. The two most important aspects of WHO are those *leading* the change and those expected to *follow* them.

- Categories 5 and 6 can be labeled CONTEXT. As such, this category can also be broken down into two convenient sets of conditions, *internal* to the organization and *external.*

- Finally, category 7 can be called the HOW of change.

As we noted earlier, the field of organizational change has been largely fix-ated on the HOW question, researching, writing, and consulting about the best processes to use when faced with change (any change). We have intentionally put this category last because, as we will demonstrate, until we consider WHAT, WHO, and the CONTEXT we won't really know what approach is best, or HOW to proceed. In fact, a careful consideration of WHO and CON-TEXT may cause us to rethink or reevaluate the WHAT (remember our deck-building example?). In extreme situations, the WHAT may even be dropped, or postponed. In other words, a different change goal may be more appropri-ate given who will be involved and what the circumstances are.

These questions, depicted in Figure 2.2, form the framework for the rest of the book. They represent the backbone of a more comprehensive way of think-

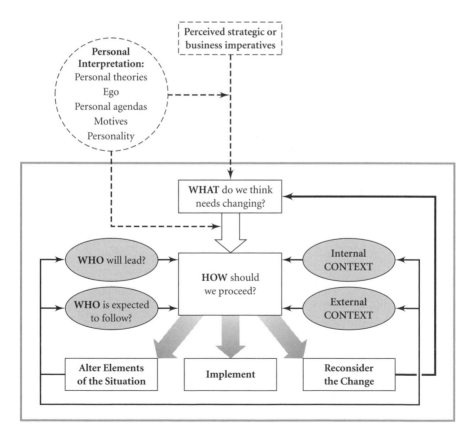

Figure 2.2. Key elements of a comprehensive change framework

ing about change, and, it is hoped, can better guide our thinking when approaching change. Such a model pushes us to view change as the complex, challenging task it is. In this framework, change leadership is about shaping a plan for change that addresses the issues of "what," while taking into account "with whom" and "under what conditions" (context) in formulating a road map for "how" to go forward. Let's look at this model more closely.

THE CHANGE MODEL

The change model itself falls within the large rectangular box in Figure 2.2. It presumes that WHAT has to change has been determined or selected, or at least considered as a first cut (earlier we noted that the choice of a change alternative may not be a straightforward question, and we will deal with this issue again in the next chapter). Thus a decision has been made to introduce a major change involving organizational systems, processes, structures, people, or business models. The white boxes and arrows down the middle represent the way change is often handled (illustrated in Figure 2.1); in other words, leaders decide WHAT they want to do, may give varying amounts of thought to HOW, and then proceed to "roll out" or implement the change.

The gray boxes and arrows represent the previously noted "missing" elements and options ignored in many treatments of change. These missing factors help explain why things so often go wrong. Here, before jumping too quickly to implementation, you consider several things. What do you know about the leader(s) being asked to carry the burden of the change effort? What do you know about the skills, motivation, morale, and other limitations or strengths of those expected to implement the change? What organizational factors, events, conditions, systems, processes, or other realities will hinder or facilitate your efforts? What is going on in the organization's external environment that may facilitate or hinder your change efforts?

The unique (and difficult) part of our framework is that it now presents us with three options: (1) Incorporate all these assessments into a better plan for HOW—in other words, our change process should, as much as possible, *account* for the various answers produced from asking these questions; (2) modify some of the elements in these categories, such as selecting different leaders, transferring in or hiring some new people; or modifying some current practices, processes, systems, or procedures before proceeding with the desired change (indicated by the thinner feedback loops); or (3) reconsider (alter or abandon) the WHAT in light of the answers to the various questions (represented by the thicker feedback loop). Better to realign your thoughts about what you want to or can actually change, bringing them into alignment with what you have to work with, than to push forward with an "ideal" change only to be sabotaged by the other elements of the situation.

Let us illustrate how the same business problem, suggesting a particular change, will result in very different change approaches. Let's say you want to reorganize a sales organization currently split along product lines into customer-based groupings. You have carefully analyzed the pros and cons of this change, and your assessment is based on a sound understanding of the business benefits of providing a more coordinated, single point of contact sales effort. Examining the major trade-offs, you've concluded that the benefits of having your best customers being called on by only one salesperson, representing the full line of products, will outweigh the potential problems of salespeople not possessing deep knowledge of all the products they represent, or favoring products they understand better and can sell more easily. So much for the WHAT, now let us proceed with two different scenarios:

1. In the first scenario, the person leading the change is a newly hired sales manager, coming in from a different industry to replace a recently retired manager. The salesforce is largely long-tenured and respected for their technical expertise. They are highly compensated for their efforts and take pride in their accomplishments and reputation. The company is doing very well, but this person was hired to "take it to the next level." The company's major competitor has recently been gaining market share, signing up some large customers, in part by offering them this type of "one-stop shopping," noting that your company does not offer it.

2. In the second scenario, the person leading this change has been promoted from within, and is generally viewed as the top salesperson in the company. He has great support among the salesforce and long-term relationships with many of them. His predecessor was fired because the company has been losing customers, while the chief competitor has been gaining market share. One major complaint from customers, seen as valid by most people in the company, has been that "the right hand doesn't know what the left hand is doing." Different

salespeople from the company sometimes bump into each other at the customer's site, and when calls come in to check on multiple-product orders, no one person seems able to provide an update on the various pieces of the order.

In each scenario, though the WHAT is the same, HOW one proceeds should be predicated on an assessment of the other considerations. In scenario 1, being the new kid on the block, and from a different industry, the leader wants to be careful not to come across as having all the answers. The salesforce is experienced and successful, suggesting that extensive involvement of the salesforce might be critical for generating the details of the reorganization and crucial for gaining their commitment. The leader might consider using the competitor's organization as a possible starting point or illustration. Even if she thinks she has thought the situation through, she might need to reconsider her first solution in light of the issues and alternatives raised during these deliberations.

Given the experience, reputation, and compensation levels of the salesforce, the leader wants to be careful not to lose their support. Given that the situation is not dire, creating a sense of "crisis" or "urgency" might not seem genuine or credible when coming from an outsider. So, basically, the leader wants to identify the business issue, use collaborative techniques to jointly solve the business problem, honor people's past accomplishments, and be sure that any new organization does not unduly threaten or alienate the salesforce, such as by negatively affecting their compensation. If need be, the leader should be prepared to make collateral changes to address such concerns, and to remove barriers she identifies as hindering any jointly derived solution.

In scenario 2, the leader's credibility is high, his rapport with the salespeople is good, the urgency is obvious, and the symptoms point in the direction of what would be an appropriate solution. The leader can now be more directive, float his proposal, provide any information that reinforces his position, ask for inputs to be sure he did not miss anything, and promise to tackle negative consequences as they are identified. The implementation process is more straightforward, the need to change is probably appreciated by most, and it is more likely that people will agree on the desired solution, as well as on the implementation plan and schedule.

Being closely identified with the sales organization, this leader may be trusted by people to be sensitive to key issues, such as the impact on compensation, and to provide credible solutions to potential problems. The leader should address how he plans to deal with potential problems and provide a mechanism for people to voice concerns that will inevitably arise. Bottom line—the WHAT in both scenarios is the same, but upon consideration of the WHO and the CONTEXT, the appropriate HOW is quite different.

In another, much publicized, example we can see how the WHAT, WHO, CONTEXT, and HOW can interact to affect outcomes, even to the point of obscuring, or leading to the misinterpretation of events and their causes. During Carly Fiorina's short and tumultuous tenure at Hewlett-Packard (HP), much of the focus was on her decision to merge HP with Compaq Computer. When things began to unravel at HP, people were quick to blame the WHAT, in other words, that it was a strategic mistake to effect the merger. Now, after her firing and HP's resurgence, people are saying the merger may not have been such a bad idea. Well, was it a poor choice of WHAT, or a much better WHAT than most people thought, but poorly implemented?

Fiorina had major blind spots concerning her "outsider" status and her leadership credibility and style, important aspects of WHO will lead. She did not assess or take stock of her followers, their long-term tenure, their engineering mind-sets, their pride in the organization and its past, and their expectations for their leaders—the followership aspect of WHO. She showed little respect for the HP culture and created unnecessary turmoil and distractions by simultaneously initiating structural and reporting changes (not to mention forgetting that the founder's son was sitting on the board)—CONTEXT factors.

Finally, she paid way too little attention to how these various factors should be incorporated in crafting a careful change implementation strategy (HOW) that would have been more likely to get her the results she wanted. Her WHAT may have been very appropriate; however, her failure to diagnose the rest of the situation and adapt her change approach accordingly proved to be her undoing.

The main point of these illustrations is to highlight the futility of jumping to "how to implement change" without first considering the other factors. The "how" has to depend on the "what," "who," and "context." Furthermore, we can even see how the "what" we want to change may have to be modified, once we consider these other factors. Treatments of change that begin and end with a focus on HOW, ignoring all of these other factors, trade simplicity (sometimes at the extreme) for realism and effectiveness.

WHAT DO WE (OR CAN WE) KNOW ABOUT
EACH ELEMENT OF THE MODEL?

By now we hope that the change model, plus the examples of how it might work, may seem like a straightforward, commonsense way of depicting the key issues involved in leading change. But if we stop and think for a moment, we've just scratched the surface in terms of potential complexities. We characterized each of the major questions the change leader should ask in terms of a few, selective dimensions or aspects. In our salesforce reorganization scenarios, we talked only about the sales manager's tenure and credibility. In the IIP case, we similarly touched on the culture, the followers, and the leader in terms of a few salient characteristics.

Surely, each of these factors can be characterized along many other dimensions. For example, wouldn't the leader's personality (for example, charismatic or not) or communication style (for example, effective or not) make a difference? Wouldn't the company's culture (for example, proud or stuck in the past), senior leadership (for example, supportive or aloof), history (good or bad track record in managing transitions), and personnel policies (for example, rewarding tenure versus merit) make a difference? Wouldn't industry trends (growth or decline), technology trends (rapidly changing or stable), and the economic environment (booming or recessionary) make a difference? Of course, they would!

In other words, under each of the categories in Figure 2.2, one can envision multiple factors that need to be considered. Which ones are the most salient? How many do you need to account for? How do you know you've entertained all the important aspects of each factor? As we've noted several times, dealing with change is a messy and challenging proposition. We can now see this messiness arising not only from the need to consider this confluence of WHAT, WHO, and CONTEXT, but also from realizing that each of these factors may be characterized along multiple dimensions. What is one to do?

Managing is the art and science of making decisions under uncertainty. If every salient aspect of a situation were known with certainty, you could program a robot, or the proverbial "trained monkey," to manage. In contrast, if nothing is known about a situation (maximum uncertainty), then you are really just gambling when you choose a response. In reality, certainty-uncertainty is not a dichotomy; rather, it is a continuum.

Some things about a change situation leaders "know" or "should know" (for example, the current information systems are not up to the job of providing the type of data that the inventory system changes will require); some things they have no way of knowing (for example, the person providing the technical leadership on the project is about to leave for another job); and some things they may not exactly "know," but should have a hunch about (for example, the software vendor has never delivered a finished project on time or within budget, so why expect it now?).

Yet managers often express "surprise" at certain outcomes even though more careful reflection would have alerted them to potential problems. In these cases, we shake our heads and think to ourselves (or say out loud to others): "What was she thinking?" or "He should have known." Thus change leadership is about moving beyond just what you think needs changing. It's about expanding your assessment of the change situation, and planning for events as you can best anticipate them, thereby improving the probability of a successful outcome.

Where do these deeper insights into what else to consider come from? First and foremost, they come from reflections upon your own experiences. What worked (or didn't), when, and why? What factors derailed previous change efforts? What did you conclude in your *post-mortems* (if you conducted them) about why things turned out the way they did? There is a great deal of personal and organizational learning associated with previous change efforts; unfortunately, people usually don't do a good enough job of capturing it and making it available for future efforts.

Another source for such insights is learning from others' experiences. If most leaders you know or have read about, who came into a new organization or situation and acted as if they knew exactly what needed changing from day one, wound up failing, why would you repeat this mistake? Yet new leaders often think change is why they were recruited and rush headlong into its murky waters, aiming to fix things others are not even sure or aware are broken.

A third source for guiding your thinking about change and its consequences is seeking evidence from both the business world and the academic world about others' experiences. For example, a great deal is known about what really happens when organizations try to implement Enterprise Resource Planning (ERP) systems. The pain and confusion are always high, the turmoil is always greater than expected, the costs are always much higher than promised, and the time required is always longer than anticipated. Yet with this knowledge widely available "on the street," executives routinely fail to account for such evidence, thinking theirs will be a different case. Just ask an assembled group of managers how their ERP implementation is going (or has gone) and note the nervous giggles and outright expressions of frustration.

Seeking additional information about aspects of WHO and CONTEXT is simply a way of reducing the uncertainty you confront—not eliminating it. Thus to focus only on how to manage change, while ignoring everything else, is to leave most or all of the outcomes to chance. To include some of the other factors, and make judgments about what dimensions of each ought to influence your thinking, will reduce such uncertainty. Not to zero, but to something more acceptable and actionable than if you did not do so, thus increasing the predictability of your outcomes. Remember, you are trying to improve your change batting average, not to bat 1.000! Thus "star" change leaders anticipate more factors, and more readily recognize where they need more information and assistance, than do mere average ones, and definitely more than do poor ones.

CONCLUSION

In this chapter we have laid out the road map we plan to use for the rest of the book. The model presented here is aimed at offering a new and different mental framework for thinking about leading significant organizational changes. It acknowledges the complexity of change situations and how they may be best addressed, while at the same time focusing on several relatively straightforward elements to guide your thinking. It also puts into perspective that HOW change should be managed, the focus of so much writing, consulting, and speculation from practitioners and academics, needs to be repositioned as one of the final steps in your change deliberations, not the centerpiece. The process to be used for implementing a given change is predicated on the thoughtful analysis of WHAT you are trying to change; WHO the leader(s) and followers are; and the CONTEXT, internal as well as external, in which the change is to take place. Given such an assessment, either we derive considerable insights into the most appropriate implementation process, or we are forced to reconsider whether or when to proceed with the contemplated change, or whether the situation should first be altered so as to make it more hospitable to the desired change.

In the next chapter, we will begin the exploration of this framework by considering issues having to do with what we think needs changing, and challenging some of the often-held assumptions about why. In subsequent chapters, we will explore the salient aspects of the other domains that need to be entertained as we make decisions about how to proceed, making change leadership less of a black box (or pure art) and more of a science.

3

WHAT IS CHANGING, AND WHERE?

"Struggling CEOs often seize on top-level corporate restructuring as a way to appease anxious boards and shareholders or to galvanize employees around the importance of change. But . . . executives are unwise to assume that restructuring is a quick fix. . . ."
McKinsey & Company report [1]

Most treatments of organizational change presume all change efforts are, theoretically at least, appropriate for the situation at hand. Thus variations in outcomes are thought to be primarily a function of the quality of change management techniques or processes used. In other words, success or failure is the result of HOW well you do it, not WHAT you are trying to do. Consequently, there is an extensive literature on "how to manage change," with no specific reference to the nature of WHAT is being implemented. Rarely does anyone stop and ask, "Why this change?" or "Which of several change options might give us the best results?" or "What would it take to successfully execute this option, and do we have what it takes?" or, heaven forbid, "What if we didn't make this (or any other) change?" In light of these questions, focusing solely on HOW to manage the change doesn't make much sense.

Toward the end of 2005, Steven Ballmer, CEO of Microsoft, announced a major reorganization. The *BusinessWeek* headline read, "Less could be more at Microsoft—Going from seven units to three may reignite the entrepreneurial fires."[2] The article noted the company's contention that collapsing seven units into three would help speed up decision making.

Microsoft had previously announced a massive makeover only a few years earlier: "Eight new divisions, each having unprecedented autonomy, aim to free Microsoft from its bureaucratic morass."[3] Expanding to eight divisions, it was touted, would reduce bureaucracy, increase autonomy, speed up decision making, and promote entrepreneurship. How can two diametrically opposed solutions, going from centralization to decentralization and back to centralization, both be in the service of the same objectives, such as speeding up decisions? Furthermore, of the things commonly recognized as frustrating Microsoft (such as product delays, too much tweaking of current products with too few "new" products, exodus of talented people to "hot" companies such as Google, and so on), structure may not be the only, or even the likeliest, place one would go looking for a fix, so why this remedy?

The McKinsey study quoted in the opening to this chapter compared forty-five underperforming global companies from different industries and across all geographies that had undergone restructuring to a control group of similarly underperforming companies that did not restructure. The researchers found that companies which resisted restructuring achieved economic recovery, in terms of total returns to shareholders, more quickly than did those that restructured. They note that those which restructured "may actually have been distracted by the shake-up of high-level functions, product groups, or geographies at a time when more pressing business imperatives needed attention."

Similarly, tactics such as layoffs or leadership changes are also frequently wielded as changes expected to fix organizations. In spite of the many warnings and the empirical evidence that companies cannot save themselves into prosperity, cost-cutting and, more specifically, layoffs are still a common "go to" tactic when performance problems arise. Yet after studying S&P 500 firms that initiated downsizing between 1982 and 2000, researchers at the University of Colorado found "no significant, consistent evidence that employment downsizing led to improved financial performance as measured by return on assets or industry-adjusted return on assets."[4]

In his book *The Disposable American,* Louis Uchitelle, the *New York Times* economics reporter, also concludes that slashing staff does not, in the long term, lead to better stock performance.[5] Furthermore, if one computes the "hidden" costs of severance, potential lawsuits, loss of institutional memory and knowledge, rehiring expenses that invariably follow, loss of trust in management, loss of goodwill in the community, and survivors who are now more risk averse and alienated, one could argue that even the short-term economics of such strategies are illusory.

Do these change techniques have merit? The answer is a definite "maybe." Each of them may be a potential solution to a particular set of problems. Responses such as reorganizations, cost-cutting, and new technologies are important change tools, but they are just that—*tools*. Too often, however, such change tools can also each be a solution looking for a problem, or the wrong solution to the right problem. What is too often overlooked is the quality of the decision process that led to the particular change being chosen, the "fit" of the chosen change with the specific organization and the setting, and the resources required (realistically) to make it happen.

TRANSLATING BUSINESS IMPERATIVES INTO WHAT TO CHANGE

Our model, presented in the previous chapter, focused on the various elements to be considered when you think a particular WHAT may be an appropriate and reasonable change goal. However, it was noted that moving from the assessment of the business situation to a particular change alternative may not be all that straightforward. The same imperative may suggest multiple solutions depending on the translation process used by the leaders. For example, on the basis of financial indicators, we may conclude something will need to be done to contain costs (a business imperative). The subsequent decision to reduce staff, consolidate certain offices, or improve business processes is simply a decision about what we think is most likely to address this imperative.

Yet in most cases, the decision of WHAT to change is treated as a given or intuitively obvious (though often it is only obvious to the one or ones proposing the change). You need to remember that the selected choice of a response is just that, a choice, even if you allow that leaders' assessments of the business imperatives are often correct. You need to recognize that the perception of business imperatives, and the subsequent translation of such perceived imperatives into change initiatives, represents a process of *interpretation* with all its attendant subjectivities. Thus, as was noted in Chapter 2, managers' personal beliefs, egos, personalities, experiences, and personal motives will all be involved.

For example, when the recently appointed CEO of Ford, Alan Mulally, used the words "even more than turnaround, I would use the word transformation . . . of the product line . . . and of the business"[6] to describe the situation he faced, everyone probably agreed that comprehensive changes were necessary. However, it is safe to bet that as he translates this overarching imperative into more concrete change plans, such agreement will diminish. Business demands or strategic imperatives do not necessarily translate easily into specific change plans, though many leaders try to convince their organizations that the current change is the only possible response.

Thus the decision to merge two organizations is often (at least partially) driven by the desire on the part of the leader to lead a larger organization (ego), by incentive systems that provide larger rewards for heading larger organizations or producing more revenue (motives), or even by personal convictions about effective business models. Billions of dollars have been lost in the search for "synergies," as shareholders of Daimler-Chrysler, Ford, and Time-Warner know only too well, while billions more will be lost going the other way, as Daimler-Chrysler has broken up, Ford is trying to sell its Luxury Car Group, and Time-Warner is being pressured to divest itself of past acquisitions.

The choice of what to change may also reflect personal biases, predispositions, and even deeply rooted and sometimes unconscious processes. When car maker Porsche bought a significant stake in Volkswagen, some attributed the decision, in part, to a Freudian wish on the part of the grandson of the founder "to lead a bigger company than my grandfather."[7]

In our own research, we have found that both the reason for most changes and the choice of the particular change were anything but obvious to those affected. In one study we conducted, involving close to eight hundred employees across thirty-one different organizations,[8] we asked employees for their perception of the extent to which the change they were experiencing was inevitable, given the realities faced by the organization.

A vast majority, 84 percent, of these respondents did not perceive the change they were experiencing as dictated by a situational or business imperative. Instead, they saw management as having had some, and at times a lot of, discretion in selecting the organization's change response. So although from a managerial perspective a change may look completely appropriate, necessary, or blatantly obvious given the circumstances, those tasked with implementing the change will quite often have very different views of why the change is occurring, views that will undoubtedly affect their motivation to support or embrace the change.

In terms of our framework, the ideal business strategy, and the changes it implies, needs to be reconsidered in light of what is known and what can be potentially found out about the change and the setting. Successful change leaders not only correctly assess and interpret the business conditions that require an adaptive response, they also realistically size up their organization's limits, capabilities, resources, and enthusiasm for enacting the adaptive response they're considering. They then blend these understandings into a unique, setting-appropriate change proposal. Thus the WHAT of change is setting-specific, which is why "copycat" changes that simply imitate what other leaders or organizations have done, or even try to replicate what one has done in a different setting, so often fail.

In our model, such considerations will cause you to either stick to your original, strategy-suggested change, focusing your attention on the implementation; replace or modify your change idea with a different approach based on what you conclude is both doable and likely to address the demands of the situation; or make other changes so as to lay the groundwork for the originally conceived change. Unfortunately, too many leaders stick to their original change idea without ever going through the deliberations proposed here. They fail to appreciate the difference between an ideal or optimal solution and a functional, realistic one. This gap between ideal and realistic becomes all the more apparent as one contemplates how the proposed change will track as it works its way down through the organization.

DISAGGREGATING THE OVERALL CHANGE

Up to this point, we've talked about generic "leaders" and "followers." That is, the "leader" was thought to be someone high enough in the organization to initiate a major change, and by default, the "followers" were everyone else. Our examples of leaders and how they handled change were largely of CEOs or other high-level executives. This is because many of the major changes in organizations do originate at these levels and, in part, because what these people do is more visible to everyone else, covered by the press, analysts, and others, and successes and failures are widely broadcast.

Yet the reality is that if change is going to occur, it has to be embraced, shaped, and led by people further down the hierarchy. Downstream leaders, however, face a reality that is different from that of their bosses. They may not have the positional power to make certain things happen; they may not be able to shape events even if they understand what it will take to make the change successful; they may need to consider the political risks associated with doing what they think is right versus what their boss decreed; and they are often totally consumed by their day-to-day responsibilities, and thus do not have much energy, or even inclination, for change leadership.

Although these leaders may not be "change strategists" in the sense of those initiating the change, they are crucial to the overall change success. They may or may not be able to be strategic in formulating their own piece of the larger change; they may or may not have a great deal of control and influence in planning and controlling their aspect of the implementation. Major changes typically involve multiple leaders, each having their own set of followers, all operating under different conditions of autonomy, resources, power, and influence.

For example, in early 2006, Intel Corporation announced a major reorganization to better address market conditions for microprocessors. Instead of focusing only on PCs, the company planned to become a player in several major fields such as consumer electronics, wireless communications, and even healthcare. This reorganization was seen as weakening the historically solid grip engineers had on the running of divisions, increasing the power of nonengineers, such as marketing types—the new CEO, Paul Otellini, being the first nonengineer to lead the company—and reducing the influence of the powerful PC group.

To better understand the implications of this reorganization, how its implementation might unfold, and what issues will need to be addressed, we have to look beyond the senior leaders who decided on the change and consider the impact of the reorganization on different units as the ramifications of the change cascade downward. If we ask engineers we will get one view of the change. Asking nonengineers, we will get another. Asking those newly hired to help spearhead the new market directions, we will get still another. Asking those who feel that their life-long commitment to the company has been betrayed by the shift away from PCs, we're likely to get a very different view.

The success of the implementation, the various costs associated with it, and any pockets of turmoil it may create are clearly a function of different levels of support, enthusiasm, cynicism, and leadership to be found in these subunits.

Whether key employees put their resumes in play may be a function of where in the organization they reside. It is this local meaning, far more so than the broader goals put forth by the change initiators, that shapes local reactions and thus the success of the change.

Let's consider a large retailer's decision to centralize purchasing for the sake of increasing quantity discounts from vendors and better managing inventory levels. This decision can now be viewed as consisting of multiple subchanges (sub-WHATs), each possibly holding the key to the ultimate success or failure of the overall effort. Each organizational subunit faces its own challenges. Corporate purchasing will have to plan for and consider the smooth transition of purchasing functions from regional centers to its own department. This may involve upgrading systems, training people, developing a better understanding of store operations, getting support from IT and other staff groups, and making sure they obtain the necessary resources.

Regional and store managers will need to deal with the impact of the change on store staff and operations. Processes will need to be reexamined and the transition to the new system planned. The impact of the new system on store operations, flexibility, response times, and inventory levels will need to be anticipated and adjustments made. The redeployment of staff currently in charge of purchasing will have to be handled, perhaps requiring coordination with the human resources department (HR). The performance and morale of store managers whose sense of autonomy and control may be eroded will need to be considered, and adjustments made to metrics and reward systems that capture outcomes no longer under their control (such as inventory management).

Finally, the various staff support organizations, such as information systems (IS) or HR, will need to consider the implication of the change for their operation, their resource allocation, their schedules, and their workloads. They will need to examine the capacity of their technical people to deliver services, manage their relationships with both the purchasing and the retail organizations, and handle the various technical aspects of the project. They also need to ask whether their leadership can exert upward influence concerning details of the change and their ability to influence those in other organizational units.

As this particular decision gets implemented, the initial WHAT (centralized purchasing) gets retranslated into multiple sub-WHATs, with the implications of these more local change aspects varying widely. Clearly, the leaders of each of these units face different leadership challenges; they've each been dealt a different hand.

AN EXAMPLE FROM THE FIELD

Working with an organization whose business strategy was to achieve very rapid growth through frequent acquisitions of smaller firms in its industry, we found one department, Finance and Accounting, experiencing the lowest morale and the highest turnover during this period of significant change—so much so that this situation was endangering the organization's ability to continue to change, because the merging of accounting systems was one of the most crucial steps in the integration of the new acquisitions.

Senior management's push to rapidly consolidate these acquisitions in order to realize the financial synergies used to justify the acquisitions in the first place resulted in incredible pressures being placed on this group. Consolidating and blending the often incompatible business systems of the acquired companies into the parent company's systems was the key to successful integration, and the Finance and Accounting department represented the bottleneck.

This situation began straining the organization's capacity to digest these acquisitions and translate them into profitable or bottom-line growth rather than just top-line growth. As people began to identify Finance and Accounting as the problem, senior management began to come down hard on them, while other departments blamed their own inability to perform their work in a timely fashion on the mess in that department. As morale in the department sank, and turnover increased, due to the tremendous workload and the not-so-subtle pressure from senior management, the department's capacity to digest the changes decreased further, threatening the entire business strategy of growth by acquisition.

We assessed the extent of change in each department, in terms of work procedure changes and disruptions, departmental members' perceptions that they were losing personal control over their work lives, the quality of the change leadership within each department, and people's commitment to the organization. Our results for the four largest departments are shown in Figure 3.1. The people in the Finance and Accounting department reported constantly having to revise their work procedures to handle the load and learn the idio-syncrasies of the newly acquired systems; they were in a constant "crisis man-agement" mode.

Furthermore, the unrealistic targets, severe time pressures, extremely long work hours, and internal turmoil in the department resulted in feelings that both their personal and work lives were spinning out of control. They also re-ported the lowest ratings of all departments for the quality of change leader-ship in their department. These dynamics resulted in the lowest organizational commitment scores of any department in the company, portending more tur-moil, decreased motivation, and increased turnover.

From this experience we can learn several important points about organiza-tional change. First, people often speak of change in terms of the strategic- or corporate-level initiative, in this case, mergers and acquisitions. To better under-stand employee reactions, we have to get closer to "where the rubber meets the road," namely, the actual impact on the different units. The turmoil, ill will, and poor performance were not caused by the change per se (that is, people do not "naturally" resist acquisitions any more so than they "naturally" resist any other type of change); rather, they were caused by the way the change was handled by leaders at the top of the organization. Low commitment, low morale, and

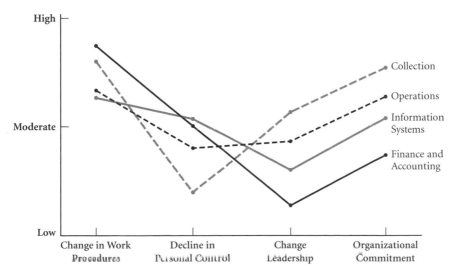

Figure 3.1. Departments experiencing the same change differently

turnover are not the natural outcomes of acquisitions. Rather, they are the result of events at the work-unit and personal levels and how these were handled.

Second, not focusing on subunit reactions, or change impact below the strategic, senior-management level, can blind you to the eventual problems that may sabotage your strategic-level initiatives. Finally, although other departments also experienced increases in pressure and decreases in personal control of about the same magnitude as Finance and Accounting, it seems that the poor state of change leadership in the latter may have caused the much more negative reactions.

This case is a good illustration of a business strategy lacking a viable change strategy. That is, little thought was given to managing the changes resulting from the implementation of the business strategy. The organization's capacity to respond, the adequacy of resources, the quality of the change plan, and the collateral changes that would need to be made were not adequately considered.

On a spreadsheet the strategy seemed like a winner. The oft-touted "synergies" seemed to be there for the picking. In reality, it turned out to be quite another story of high hopes, bungled integrations, disappointed shareholders, and turmoil in the executive suite, as well as elsewhere in the organization. To a large extent, one subunit, and senior leadership's failure to plan for and address issues in that subunit, was enough to derail the overall corporate strategy. A strategy in the absence of effective change strategizing often becomes merely a pipe dream.

WHAT'S THE CHANGE LEADER TO DO?

Those who initiate a change need to realize that changes of any significance need to be disaggregated into the component parts that will cascade down through the organization. More important, leaders need to understand that overall success is directly related to how well the component pieces are then reaggregated. Change leaders must fully consider the cascading subchanges, potential bottlenecks, and key junctures for the change the way we did for the corporate purchasing example. Next, they also need to identify the key leadership roles along the way, think about the demands placed on these various, downstream leaders, and assess the current incumbents' capacity (personal and situational) to perform these roles.

When considering the role of downstream change leaders and their work units, change initiators further need to be aware that orientations toward the change idea, along with the motivation and capacity to support it, will vary greatly in different levels and parts of the organization. The grand vision of the strategists becomes much less salient and compelling as mid-level change leaders make decisions about their own contributions and try to get rank-and-file followers to support the change.

Plotting the course of the change as it moves downstream, leaders can begin to formulate a change plan that is more consistent with local realities. Going back to our Finance and Accounting department debacle described earlier, had senior leaders properly determined what the disaggregation of the growth-by-acquisition change strategy might look like as it rolled through the organization, they would have been able to develop a very different approach.

They could have better identified the load that would be placed on the Finance and Accounting department. This could have alerted them to engage the department head and key employees in their planning. Having done so, they may have reconsidered how many acquisitions, of what size, and over what time period the department could digest. This could have resulted in an assessment of alternatives, such as augmenting the department with additional resources to help with the transitions, considering the tailoring of the business strategy to their change capacity, or even assessing the department head's ability to lead such changes in his department. Instead, the business strategy was pursued "full speed ahead," and the implementation was seen as "their" problem. Unfortunately, it became everybody's problem.

THE ROLES OF DOWNSTREAM LEADERS

We've asked hundreds of mid-level and upper-mid-level managers to identify a particular change they've been involved in and answer the following questions:

- Whose idea was it?
- Who decided the timing of the change?
- Who did the planning for the change?
- Who had responsibility for implementing the change?

Although the vast majority of the managers reported significant responsibility for change implementation, from the patterns of answers to the first three questions, we've identified three prototypical change leadership situations for downstream leaders.

Implementation leaders typically receive "marching orders" from the strategic leader as to the broad parameters of the desired change (for example, reduce costs by 10 percent), but enjoy a great deal of discretion as to how to go about it. In fact, these leaders are free to do their own change strategizing and come up with the appropriate WHAT for their units and plan the implementation. We usually find such leaders at levels of the organization that also typically have reasonable autonomy as to other aspects of running the business, for example, business unit heads, department heads, or heads of major functions such as engineering or manufacturing.

Process leaders typically do not have the latitude enjoyed by implementation leaders, but they do enjoy a great deal of latitude around the details of the implementation process (the HOW). Sometimes these leaders may be able to gently influence the WHAT, or make modifications to the WHO and the CONTEXT. This may result from their being asked for inputs, or from their lobbying with strategic or implementation leaders. By and large, however, they are tasked with figuring out how to make it happen.

Change functionaries are those who are essentially reactive to the change that has been handed them, having (or seeing themselves as having) little or no choice or influence as to the key elements of the WHAT, WHO, CONTEXT, and even HOW—they simply follow orders.

Not surprisingly, implementation leaders generally report higher levels of success for the particular change than do those in the other two roles. This may be because their perceptions of success are skewed due to the control they have over the change, a self-serving bias. We find, however, that as involvement in the planning increases, even if it's just about matters of timing, leaders feel that they have done a better job and are happier with the results. As leaders have the opportunity to join in on the decision about the nature of the change, they are more positive about the outcomes. Leaders who control their own change destiny, that is, decide on the change and are heavily involved in the planning and implementation, express the greatest satisfaction with the way things turned out.

From these observations we may conclude the following:

- Change initiators would do well to involve their potential implementers early on in the process, perhaps sharing responsibility for the actual determination of what to change, the implementation plan, and its timing.
- Not being able to control the timing or "roll out" of a change is a major frustration for those who have implementation responsibility, perhaps even more so than not being involved in other phases of the planning process.
- Downstream leaders who feel they had input into the initiation and planning stages feel better about having the responsibility for the change, and about the outcomes.
- Those who have the most control over the change initiation and implementation planning are the most optimistic about the outcomes.
- Those charged with the change need not have total control over the change and its planning, just a legitimate sense of involvement, in order to feel better about how things went.
- The combination of low involvement in initiating, planning, and deciding on timing plus high levels of responsibility for implementation is the most difficult for downstream leaders to handle.

Clearly, downstream leaders who inherit a portion of a major change initiative are often faced with significant challenges because each affected unit is faced with a unique WHAT and its own unique situation. Therefore, change initiators need to carefully consider the role to be taken by each of the downstream change leaders. Conversely, downstream leaders need to carefully weigh their options when drawn into a change conceived by others. As much as they can, they need to try to be a part of the planning, at least as far as it affects their units, including the nature of the change, the timing, the resources it will take, and the hurdles to be overcome. They need to negotiate a clear role for themselves and their work group, defining what will be required of them, when it will be required, and how their other responsibilities will be affected. These downstream leaders also need to reach agreement about their authority to seek assistance from others in the organization or any parties outside the organization, such as vendors, and what they can expect by way of support from their superiors.

CONCLUSION

This chapter highlighted several important considerations guiding the choice of WHAT to change. First, there is no one best way to address a business imperative. There are no magic bullets, and certainly reorganizations, layoffs, or other commonly used approaches for addressing business imperatives have not shown themselves to be "the answer." Second, business imperatives, or strategic concerns, do not automatically have a corresponding change solution. We cannot proceed on an "if this is the demand placed on the business, then this change is the one, and only one, which must be made" basis. The change strategy needs to be carefully tailored to both the business needs and the change situation. Third, in order to create a good fit between the business imperative and the change solution, the assessment of the change situation needs to be fairly extensive.

Finally, our framework, and the supporting field evidence, point to the importance of considering the impact and meaning of a change within all of the affected subunits. Only then can we perform a sort of "triage" to identify hot spots where things are not going well and where additional attention or resources need to be provided.

To assume change is just change is just change, regardless of where it is in the organization or who is going to implement it, is a recipe for disaster. Similarly, to assume that senior leadership is the only leadership level that really counts and that the positional power and strong will of senior leaders is enough to ensure a change's success as it cascades down through the organization tends to be foolhardy and helps explain why so many changes go awry.

4

LEADING OTHERS

THROUGH CHANGE

"[Larry] Summers [the recently deposed president of Harvard University] had a great vision for Harvard that would likely have allowed it to thrive in a changing world. But what he never quite got is that leaders—especially those who are change agents—can only succeed when they have a reservoir of goodwill that allows them to convince followers that their fates are correlated."
Warren Bennis[1]

In contemplating WHAT to change, and HOW we might go about it, our change model suggests that careful attention needs to be paid to WHO will be involved—both leaders and followers. In this chapter and the next we will focus on the leader, while subsequent chapters will address follower considerations.

The notion of leadership is central to much of our thinking about organizational success and has been the subject of as much or more speculation, writing, and research as any other topic in the organizational sciences. Without (good) leadership, the success of any mission is deemed far less likely, or, in some situations, even impossible. The role of leaders is to provide direction, to motivate followers to exert the effort necessary to achieve organizational objectives, and to support or enable such efforts. At no time is this function more important than when trying to motivate organizational members to embrace and work toward a new state.

Leading implies change, and change implies leadership! In the oft-heard distinction between managing and leading, made popular by Harvard professor Abraham Zaleznik, the smooth running of day-to-day affairs, through the design and enforcement of organizational systems, processes, and procedures, is seen to be the domain of *managers*. Setting direction, enlisting people's help in moving toward a new goal, and being willing and able to alter human and economic relationships represent the work of *leaders*.

Managing and leading are both embodied in the *change leader*. Change leadership is not only about setting new directions. Although it does often require the articulation of a future vision, it is also about properly setting the stage, making convincing arguments, developing a reasonable plan, being realistic about resources, assessing capabilities, and attending to execution details. In other words, it is about applying the change framework we are proposing, thus taking into account the interplay between the nature of the change, the cast of characters expected to lead and enact it, and the situation in which it is to take place.

A change vision not in line with situational realities or one with a poor plan for execution is simply a hallucination. This is so no matter how carefully the words are crafted; how passionately they are conveyed; or whether they are hung from a banner, printed on posters, or inscribed on laminated pocket cards for everyone to carry. A change that focuses on the right tactical details but fails to grab people's attention or ignite a desire to change course is also not likely to succeed. Ultimately, it is not only knowing what needs to be done (a necessary but not sufficient starting point), but also how to do it that is the mark of the change leader. It is the inspiration and perspiration of the leader that will motivate followers to support and work on behalf of change.

Witness Carly Fiorina's disastrous tenure at Hewlett-Packard (HP); as we noted earlier, her vision for the Compaq merger is looking better all the time. As a result of her efforts, HP is now a major force in the PC world, its traditional channels of distribution are doing very well in the important overseas and laptop markets, and its performance has successfully challenged and surpassed Dell. Unfortunately, her flamboyance, charisma, whirlwind schedule of appearances, and press coverage were not enough to carry the day. According to various press reports, her structural changes were confusing, she did not hold people accountable, she was not on top of operational issues that needed attention (nor did she heed advice to put someone on her leadership team who was), she did not establish credibility with the rest of the organization, she was not respectful of HP's culture, and she was not open to feedback from her board.[2] She may have been a great strategic thinker, even a visionary, but from all appearances she was a poor change leader.

HOW DO LEADERS MOTIVATE CHANGE?

There are two basic reasons why followers do what they do at the behest of leaders: they feel they *want to*, or they feel they *have to*. These are not totally independent—most of us have experienced some combination of the two when dealing with a particular leader—but one is usually the primary motivator. We might further distinguish the two by saying the primary mechanisms leaders rely on are *compliance* (or even coercion) versus *persuasion* (or personal credibility).

Compliance is associated with the leader's exercise of the reward and punishment powers inherent in the position, giving subordinates little choice but to comply or risk incurring significant personal costs. When relying on persuasion, leaders get followers to adopt the desired behaviors because they want to, or because they believe it is the right thing to do. This may be because followers have confidence in the expertise of the leader, strongly identify with the leader or what the leader stands for, or have a trust-based relationship with the leader.

Although compliance and persuasion may both be ways of motivating behavior, and some might even argue it doesn't matter why people follow directives, as long as they do, they are not equal in their consequences or effectiveness. This is especially so when compliance is sought through the unbridled *and unwelcome* use of positional power. Seeking compliance through coercive means has several negative consequences.

First, for compliance to be effective, behaviors have to be closely monitored. This is not always possible, and even when it is, it consumes leaders' time and energy that might be more productively used in other endeavors. Second, leaders have to be very exacting in defining the desired behaviors, lest people comply with the letter of the request but not with the spirit ("But I did *exactly* what you told me to do!"). Third, mere compliance implies minimum acceptable performance and denies the leader the benefits of the creativity and experience of followers that might shape or improve the desired outcomes. Such "above and beyond" contributions are often the markers of successful changes.

Finally, extracting compliance usually results in negative emotional reactions, such as resentment, stress, fear, distrust, perceived loss of control, and anxiety, which may lead to various negative consequences, now or later. At one level, such emotions may interfere with the desired behaviors, rendering them less effective. At another level, they may create dysfunctional consequences such as passive-aggressive behaviors; active resistance; aggression toward other employees, customers, or vendors; withdrawal from the organization (temporary, as in absenteeism, or permanent, as in turnover); or damaging public relations (as in today's widely publicized employee blogs that can quickly place organizations in a negative light).

In some situations, such as during a crisis (to be discussed in the next chapter), followers may not mind such exercise of power; they may actually welcome it. This is especially true if the leader is seen as being able to address the crisis, protect followers from internal or external threats, or otherwise be instrumental in helping followers attain personal goals (such as financial success).

We are not naive about the role that power plays in leader-follower relationships, nor about the prevalence of the coercive use of positional power as a means for seeking compliance with change directives. However, all things being equal (for example, there is no perception of a crisis), we need to be mindful of the implications of such influence attempts on employees' willingness to embrace and support a given change initiative.

Thus it is no accident that Warren Bennis, in the quote at the opening of this chapter, talks of reservoirs of "goodwill" that allow leaders to "convince" followers. He is clearly talking about leaders with personal credibility who get others to *want* to support a change. So what are these reservoirs of "goodwill" and how do change leaders acquire them?

LEADERS' SOURCES OF PERSONAL CREDIBILITY

In addition to any compliance leaders may expect from others as a function of the positional power that may be associated with their rank and title, leaders gain personal credibility with followers from two primary sources: (1) what they do—their day-to-day actions and interactions, and (2) what they are—their public persona, reputation, and demeanor.

What Leaders Do

First and foremost, leaders persuade followers to embrace change on the basis of the strength of the *interpersonal credibility* they enjoy with those being asked to change. That is, over time (and probably over many changes), different leaders have developed qualitatively different relationships with their followers. These relationships are characterized by levels of mutual support and mutual need—satisfaction that will affect followers' inclinations to move in the direction the leader suggests. Followers will do so to the extent they trust that the leader will not steer them wrong, believe the leader has thought things through reasonably well, will involve them when and where appropriate, has the competence and resources to pull it off, and will be supportive throughout the change effort. In such situations, the leader enjoys a degree of personal credibility or trust that motivates followers to respond positively to change attempts.

In other words, many leadership behaviors thought to be associated with good change leadership (such as involving others, communicating, listening, supporting, and so on), are really what we normally think of as good leadership practices. This represents the most potent reservoir of goodwill a leader can draw upon during a change. Conversely, the absence of such credibility, due to lack of history with followers or poor relationships with them, may be a major impediment to a leader's ability to lead change. In fact, it is poor interpersonal credibility that causes many leaders to resort to the exercise of positional power, *demanding* compliance with their change directives. It is one thing to lead change when you enjoy high-quality relationships with followers; it is another thing to do so when you are still in the process of establishing such relationships; it is quite another to do so when the quality of such relationships is damaged.

So what about leaders who don't have a history with their followers, perhaps because they are new to the organization (often having been brought in precisely to lead a change); or, while they are not new to the setting, they have come from a different area or function such that they have not yet established credibility with those they are expected to lead? These leaders need to first shape the trust relationship through early interactions with followers; they need to be change savvy.

Change-savvy leadership involves

- Careful entry into the new setting
- Listening to and learning from those who have been there longer (respecting the history and culture)

- Engaging in fact finding and joint problem solving
- Carefully (rather than rashly) diagnosing the situation
- Forthrightly addressing people's concerns
- Being enthusiastic, genuine, and sincere about the circumstances sur-
  rounding the change
- Obtaining buy-in for what needs fixing
- Developing a credible plan for making that fix

In change leadership, as in so many other interactions, first impressions are important, and we only get to make them once. The savvy change leader uses early encounters to begin the relationship-building process, laying the groundwork for increased interpersonal credibility that, over time, will form the foundation for long-term trust.

Of course, leaders already enjoying sound interpersonal relationships with followers can also benefit from aspects of savvy change leadership. That is, much of what is written about how to lead change really addresses "dos" and "don'ts" such as listening, being open to inputs, obtaining buy-in, jointly diagnosing problems, encouraging, developing a road map, and celebrating successes. Thus the savvy change leadership reservoir can supplement the interpersonal credibility reservoir, increasing the leader's capacity to influence followers to adopt the change.

What Leaders Are

Leaders, especially those new to a situation, may also possess sources of credibility that do not depend on personal interaction with followers. These sources are part of the leader's public persona and are used by followers to size up the leader and make personal decisions about exerting energy on behalf of a change. The two most obvious such sources are *charisma* and *reputation.* Charisma is the ability to inspire a particular view of the future, or appeal to some deep-rooted sense of values or emotions such that followers want to exert effort on behalf of the cause, sometimes even making personal sacrifices in order to do so. Reputation refers to being seen as an expert either in the technical or business aspects of the change being contemplated, or in change leadership in general.

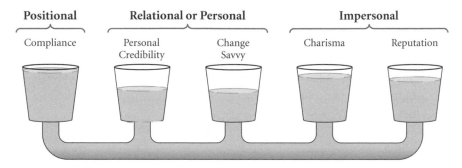

Figure 4.1. Reservoirs of influence that change leaders can draw on

That is, the leader may be known as "one of the best operations guys we have (or out there)," or the leader may have "successfully led the turnaround (or implementation or transition) at so-and-so division or company."

Figure 4.1 depicts these different reservoirs of goodwill as buckets that may be filled to different levels. In terms of relative potency, personal interactions are more powerful in influencing followers' behavior. That is, one's day-to-day experience working with a leader is a more personal, experiential, and important determinant of change experiences and change reactions than are reputation or charisma. As a new player, having the advantage of charisma, reputation, or both is nice, but will be quickly overshadowed if not supplemented by change-savvy behaviors aimed at achieving quick results and forming longer-lasting relationships. For the incumbent, the quality of the existing relationship already reflects followers' perceptions of the leader's charisma and reputation.

DRAWING ON OUR BUCKETS OF INFLUENCE

So what can we make of these different sources of influence over followers' behaviors? First of all, they are not mutually exclusive. In fact, successful change leaders may typically draw on more than one bucket or reservoir of goodwill. Second, we need to realize that buckets are interconnected, for better or worse. For example, overreliance on the compliance bucket may drain one's interpersonal credibility bucket, as well as one's reputation. Conversely, savvy change leadership is likely to fill one's personal credibility and reputation buckets.

We should also note that although all these buckets may be drawn down or replenished, they do so at different rates and with different degrees of difficulty.

Excessive reliance on compliance as an influence tactic may quickly damage one's position power, as the negative reactions of those being influenced begin to reflect in the performance and morale of the organization, thereby reducing the influence of the leader. It may also destroy relationships that may have been built over time and create a deficit from which it is difficult to recover. Similarly, as we noted earlier, charisma and reputation, both of which can precede or accompany a leader new to a situation, may quickly dwindle as a source of influence as followers assess the leader's day-to-day behaviors and make decisions about the leader's approach to change, trustworthiness, sincerity, and collegiality.

Thus, possessing strong interpersonal credibility and the display of change savvy are the most potent and enduring buckets of goodwill—charisma and reputation are the icing on the cake. Strong leader-follower relationships will be weakened if the leader repeatedly violates the "psychological contract," or the expectations of followers. However, should such leaders merely miss a step when leading a change, for example, fail to communicate something effectively, forget to include someone in a decision, or unintentionally mess something up, it may not be a big deal. Followers provide a great deal of latitude to leaders they trust.

The existence of strong interpersonal relationships usually reflects the presence of two-way communication, joint problem-solving, and mutual support. This makes it less likely that major problems will arise during a change, and more likely they will be appropriately addressed if they do. Drawing this bucket down a bit will not be disastrous. For such leaders, the ability to draw on this bucket is likely to trump their ability to draw on the other buckets as forces for change.

For the outsider coming into a change situation who cannot draw on established relationships, being change savvy is the most important quality because it begins the process of relationship building. That is, savvy change leadership is, in essence, good leadership applied to a new setting. The new leader is making deposits in the relationship bucket while carefully and sensitively navigating the specifics of change.

IS PERSONAL CREDIBILITY OR
CHANGE SAVVY MORE POTENT?

Interestingly, the literature on change leadership focuses on change-specific behaviors, such as communicating the change, creating a sense of urgency, and so on, but does not tie these behaviors into the broader, more commonly used typologies used to describe leadership styles. Conversely, the leadership literature, both academic and practitioner, focuses on sets of leader behaviors, or styles, that cut across situations, without tying these leadership styles to how a leader handles a specific change.

Recently, we set out to study the relative impact or contribution of how a leader handled a particular change (that is, how change savvy the leader was), and of the leader's general leadership styles, on followers' commitment to work on behalf of a specific change.[3] We used the popular conceptualization of transformational leadership, thought to reflect leaders' ability to create a common vision, empower followers to pursue that vision, and motivate them by virtue of the leaders' personal credibility. We then examined whether followers who reported they worked for more transformational leaders also reported that these leaders were savvier when it came to the handling of a particular change initiative.

Furthermore, we wanted to know if followers' commitment to support a particular change had more to do with how they felt about the leader in general, or with how the leader handled the specific change effort. Studying over 340 people involved in thirty different changes across different types of organizations, we found the following:

- Being viewed as a transformational leader, in general, was not automatically related to being viewed as doing a good job on any one particular change. That is, good leaders do not necessarily exhibit more appropriate, change-specific behaviors, nor are leaders who perform well vis-à-vis a particular change perceived as being more transformational.

- When followers reported that they worked for leaders who were not particularly transformational, they reported higher commitment to the change

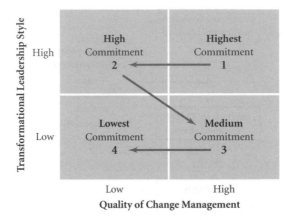

Figure 4.2. Followers' commitment to a change under different combinations of leaders' style and change-specific behaviors

when these leaders engaged in specific, change-appropriate behaviors than when they did not. However (and it's a big however), transformational leadership trumped good change leadership. That is, such leaders got more commitment to the change from their followers even when their change leadership was flawed than their weak leadership counterparts were able to get with good change leadership (see Figure 4.2).

From this research, we conclude that a good old-fashioned emphasis on developing leadership skills may be the best reservoir of goodwill one can have when leading change. When one does not enjoy such credibility, or has not had the opportunity to develop it, careful attention to change leadership principles in terms of the immediate change at hand can save the day and provide opportunities for building the longer-term, more stable relationships. Leaders who possess personal credibility will enjoy support for a particular change they are leading even if they don't quite do everything "by the book" when it comes to change management practices (although we should note that if these change-related behaviors are clumsy, inappropriate, or not seen as mutually beneficial they will drain the credibility bucket, making future changes more difficult). Absent such credibility, good change management practices are the next best thing for gaining such support.

FOLLOWERS' PERCEPTIONS OF LEADERS' BEHAVIORS DURING CHANGE

Even though personal credibility trumped change-savvy behaviors in the study just described, change-specific leadership behaviors are still important for two reasons. First, not all leaders enjoy strong credibility with their followers (or have had a chance to develop it), such that they can leverage it during a change. How they handle the change at hand will make or break them. Second, even those who do have such credibility can supplement the motivational power of their relationships with more situation-specific, change-appropriate behaviors.

In another study, we were interested in leaders' and followers' perceptions of how leaders handled specific aspects of a change, and how those perceptions were related to different change outcomes, both personal and organizational. We studied these questions using a format generally known as 360° feedback, widely used in leadership development to study observers' perceptions of leaders and their behaviors. Instead of assessing generic leader behavior, however, as most such instruments do, we developed a format asking leaders and followers to focus on a particular change and assess the extent to which the leader engaged in several change-related behaviors associated with being change savvy.

The behaviors of interest were related to different stages of the change process, assessing things leaders do to facilitate launching a change (communicate the vision, create a sense of urgency); smoothing the implementation—being sensitive to social issues (being fair, seeking inputs) and providing support (providing resources, role modeling); and sustaining the effort (providing feedback, celebrating short-term wins). In addition to rating the leadership behaviors, we also asked leaders and their followers to provide their overall ratings of the success of the change project.

Figure 4.3 shows the pattern of findings for a group of thirty-one leaders and more than three hundred of their subordinates from a large division of a Fortune 10 company. Looking at this figure, we can gain several insights into change leadership. First, we notice that for launch and the two sets of implementation behaviors (social and support), leaders exhibit somewhat of a "blind spot," that is, they think they are doing a better job than their subordinates think they are. This blind spot carries over to the assessment of how successful the change was, with leaders being far more (wildly?) optimistic than their subordinates.

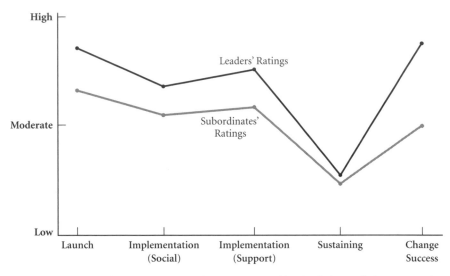

Figure 4.3. Leaders' and subordinates' assessments of leaders' change behaviors and project success

The data for the sustaining phase are interesting in that they seem to reflect good agreement on the part of the two groups that leaders do not do a lot to nurture the change once it's on the way. Leaders do not spend much time assessing change progress, providing feedback, providing "pats on the back," or other celebratory behaviors. This bias was confirmed by the change leaders in subsequent discussions, with a group consensus that "we don't do much of that around here." Thus this may be a cultural bias rather than the predisposition of the individual leaders. Unfortunately, we see this pattern all too often.

Furthermore, from the point of view of the followers, they also see the change as being far less successful than do their leaders. Suffering the stress of an unsuccessful change (as discussed in Chapter 1) can be a real demotivator, especially if this is the umpteenth time this has happened. This becomes an important leadership concern when leaders think they have deeper reservoirs of goodwill based on *their* perceptions of how the change went, and it turns out followers don't quite see it that way. Instead of "That went great, now what's next?" the leader may be greeted with "Look what you did *to* us the last couple of times!" This is another example of what we call (see Chapter 7) the "observer" bias: things look easier from the point of view of those who don't have to do them. As a result, leaders often don't fully understand the difficulties experienced by others struggling with the change. This can contribute to the creation of a gulf between leaders and followers.

From this research, we conclude the following:

1. Leaders and followers can meaningfully distinguish distinct leader behaviors associated with different phases of a change project.

2. Too few leadership behaviors are focused on sustaining the change (the only thing agreed upon by leaders and followers).

3. Leaders tend to have blind spots about the different change leadership behaviors they exhibit.

4. Leaders can have very serious blind spots about how a change really turned out, at least when compared with followers' perceptions.

These findings can be used to help us develop an understanding of the importance of focusing on change leadership behaviors in general and behaviors during specific phases of a change project in particular. They also alert leaders to seek confirmation from others so as to validate personal assessments of both personal effectiveness and project success. Having blind spots in these two areas will deny leaders opportunities for improvement, as well as mislead them about how things are going. Finally, these findings alert leaders to the importance of tracking the personal outcomes experienced by followers, in this case, change success and stress, so as to have a sense of the extent to which followers may be experiencing difficulties, building up resistance, or otherwise failing to embrace the change effort.

CONCLUSION

In this chapter we have begun to tackle the WHO portion of our framework, focusing on the leader. Here we addressed the basic mechanisms by which leaders influence followers. Using the metaphor of "buckets," we discussed how the leverage leaders enjoy when attempting to influence followers to support a change may originate from different sources. Thus leaders need to understand where their influence comes from and the implications, limitations, or advantages associated with such sources. Leadership influence is a precious commodity, and one should be careful to cultivate and not squander it.

This discussion is meant to encourage both personal and corporate intro-spection about change leadership issues. What are your strengths and weak-nesses as they apply to leading change? Have some of your approaches to change netted unsatisfactory results for one or more of the reasons described here? What about the people you work with or for? Have you been on the re-ceiving end of mismanaged or poorly led change, and do you now better un-derstand what happened? Do you understand that regardless of the positional power you enjoy, it may not be enough to achieve long-term change success?

Are you committed to soliciting and processing feedback about your own change leadership, expanding your understanding of change issues, and putting together a development plan for improvements in this area? Do you understand the way leaders build and leverage their influence to create positive change?

The successful change leader dips into as many buckets of influence as are available and uses the combination to encourage, challenge, and demand change-appropriate behaviors. Furthermore, the successful change leader pays close at-tention to the launch, implementation, and sustaining of the particular change effort. The inability to leverage interpersonal relationships with followers, cou-pled with the failure to execute change-appropriate behaviors, has oftentimes doomed change prospects.

5

LEADERS DON'T ALL LEAD
FROM THE SAME PLACE

"I spent nine months with a piece of tape on my mouth."
Maureen Chiquet, newly appointed global CEO of French design house Chanel[1]

In the previous chapter we discussed the leader's ability to influence others during change. We pointed out the fact that the availability of some influence reservoirs is situationally determined. For example, personal credibility is not available to the newcomer in a setting, and one's reputation is often not as salient if earned in an unrelated field or industry. Even the exercise of positional power and its consequences is probably dependent on organizational culture, norms, and traditions. Although in a later chapter we will address situational factors affecting one's ability to effectively lead change (the CONTEXT aspect of our change framework), in this chapter we will deal with two important and interdependent situational contingencies critical to the understanding of leadership influence—whether one is an insider or an outsider to the setting, and the urgency of the situation.

In the preceding discussions, we have placed a great deal of importance on the strength of leader-follower relationships; however, these are not typically available to leaders coming into a new situation. So it would seem that organizations would be wise to select change leaders who have already established such relationships. Yet frequently, when organizations seem to experience the greatest need to change, they associate the current state with the failures of current leadership. This triggers the importation of a new leader or leaders from the outside, often referred to as "agents for change."

THE OUTSIDER AS CHANGE LEADER

This new knight on a white horse is supposed to bring new skills to the situation; have a new and different perspective; not be bound by the current environment, culture, or assumptions; and be free of close personal or historical ties that may constrain his or her options. Thus a paradox exists in which organizations often look to rapid and successful change from those who have one hand tied behind their back—lack of interpersonal credibility with those they need to lead. What is one to do under these circumstances? One of the answers has already been provided in the last chapter—focus heavily on the approach to change, be change savvy. The other answers have to do with the degree to which one can leverage charisma or reputation and the urgency of the situation.

Although one's initial assumption may be that during crises people are more motivated to accept leadership of any kind, even these situations can be tricky. Who is it that perceives a crisis? Often, when key decision makers perceive a crisis that causes them to bring in an "agent of change," this perception is not shared by the rest, or most, of the organization's members. Furthermore, the sense of crisis is often filtered by the strength of the culture.

Those who are part of a strong, proud culture, even when facing difficulties, may downplay the crisis, be overly confident they can prevail, and have difficulty accepting the outsider as the appropriate agent of change. Such cultures may also be more sensitive to, and resentful of, cultural violations on the new leader's part. People in such cultures may also infer that the new leader's arrival implies that they are not as good as they think they are, perhaps motivating them to further dig in their heels. Under these conditions, seeking compliance through the exercise of positional power can have serious downsides, regardless of how successful one may have been in previous leadership roles. What some may have hoped would be a white horse, organizational members can greet as the proverbial Trojan Horse. Imagine the response of Home Depot executives attending the meeting at which, according to a former senior executive, the new CEO proclaimed, "You guys don't know how to run a f—ing business."[2]

Faced with a new setting, the change leader needs to be careful to be change savvy. This means taking the time to learn about the organization and the business, addressing the crisis through joint problem solving with those whose cooperation will be needed to make any changes, relying on any reputational or charismatic credits he or she can muster to initiate the process, and judiciously applying positional power to make incremental changes that build the "change savvy" and "personal credibility" reservoirs. Where the crisis is widely perceived, the culture is weakened by the crisis, and the leader brings a strong reputation or charisma to the setting, followers may willingly accept and comply with strong doses of positional power. This is especially so if the leader demonstrates a good understanding of the situation or delivers quick successes indicating that a turnaround may be at hand—evidence of a well-deserved reputation.

Carlos Ghosn, CEO of Nissan Motor Company, came in as a total outsider not only organizationally but also culturally. Lebanese-born and coming from a French company, Renault, he was put in charge of a Japanese company. His reputation was not exactly one of being warm and fuzzy, and he was described as "ruthless," having "the subtlety of a chain saw," having enormous ambition, and saddled with the label "*le cost killer*" from previous assignments.[3] Yet he is largely credited with transforming and saving Japan's number two carmaker.

Why? Because when Ghosn arrived, in 1999, the company had just lost $6.5 billion for the year, was reeling under $19 billion in debt, was rapidly losing market share, and had its survival in question. Under such conditions, Ghosn's total dedication to the cause, strong work ethic, and convincing manner represented a personal swagger or charisma he could trade on. His reputation for results at Renault and Michelin preceded him, and apparently this reputation was well-deserved, as he quickly made changes that yielded results. Given his ability to inspire, his reputation for results in the auto industry, and followers' readiness for someone to come in and rescue them from a dire situation, Ghosn's exercise of his position power, though not subtle, yielded welcomed improvements and was embraced.

Another example of a strong reputation within an industry paving the way for an outside leader to turn around an organization in crisis is William Bratton's success with several police departments, namely Boston, New York City, and Los Angeles. In each of these cases, morale and performance before his arrival were low, and his unorthodox methods and staunch support of his troops resulted in quick successes that he built on throughout his tenure. Relevant reputation or experience, a dose of charisma, plus crisis, plus results equals change success.

Lou Gerstner, at IBM, though he also came in during a widely agreed-upon period of serious difficulties for the computer giant, could not draw on the same reservoirs of influence as Ghosn or Bratton. He was not particularly charismatic; did not (or could not) rely on reputation, having come from consumer products and consulting backgrounds; and had no technology background. He was entering a culture that was very proud of its technology tradition. Given his predicament, Gerstner displayed a good amount of change savvy by disappointing those expecting a pronouncement of a grand vision for the company, choosing instead to keep his eyes and ears open.

He understood that his status as an outsider to both the company and the industry meant he did not have much street credibility. He chose to put his ear to the ground, get the pulse of the place, identify obvious fixes, and build his relationships, and eventually he presided over one of the most successful corporate transformations ever. In the absence of preexisting relationships, a strong reputation, and charisma, Gerstner did the only thing he could do—focus on careful change management (change savvy) coupled with his positional power.

Andrea Jung, when she came in as CEO at Avon, also came from a different industry into a company with diminishing prospects. What was the first thing she did? She began to sell cosmetics door-to-door as an Avon Lady. This allowed her to hear feedback about the company and its products, to empathize with the situation confronted by her salesforce, and to begin to understand what was wrong. It also helped her gain street credibility with her followers. It was only after she took the time to understand that she began making changes, leading the company to a major turnaround.

Having looked at how four leaders brought from the outside succeeded under crisis conditions, using different approaches and influence reservoirs depending on their backgrounds, let's look at one that did not succeed. Richard Thoman was brought to Xerox from IBM, where he was CFO, to become CEO. The company was widely recognized as having missed the digital transformation of office products, having mishandled competition from Japanese copiers, and suffering from an insular and arrogant culture. Yet who was this man the board thought would be an effective agent of change? He was an intellectual, having four advanced degrees, including a Ph.D. Thoman has been described as a "perpetual outsider"; as not connecting well enough with people "to get a feel for what was going on"; and as "overbearingly blunt in his criticism," "all but incapable of small talk," "haughty," "not really a warm person," and a "charm-challenged brainiac [who] was a bad fit."[4]

With all this going for him, Thoman declared himself "more of a leader, someone who can size up a situation and act on it quickly." And act he did. "While everyone likes to be liked, for me it was more important to get things done."[5] Thoman proceeded to force a pace of change the company simply could not digest. Unfortunately, he was not well-enough connected to the people around him to realize this. Tempers flared, support flagged, support from key executives was lost, and finally the board removed him.

These illustrations help us develop more general principles concerning leadership influence sources and their effectiveness under different change-related situations. When things are going poorly, organizations look to leadership to reverse course, often from the outside. If the leader has a reputation suggesting she can do so, or the charisma to convince followers she can, she is likely to get a chance to prove it. If the reputation is salient for fixing the problem at hand, and quick successes follow, the reputational reservoir will continue to fill, relationships may be established as followers begin to trust the leader to get them out of the mess, and the exercise of positional power will be accepted on the basis of improvements in people's prospects and outcomes.

If a new leader lacks reputation, charisma, or both, followers expect him or her to first get the lay of the land, to seek their expertise as long-tenured members of the organization, and to demonstrate sensitivity for the setting and the culture. If this approach yields improvements in the organization's prospects, these leaders will quickly enjoy a filling of their "change savvy" and "personal credibility" reservoirs, which will make further changes much easier.

For such leaders, relying on the exercise of positional power alone, simply because they possess it, is likely to prove problematic. The exercise of power, coupled with lack of change savvy (in the absence of reputation or charisma), yields personal upheaval, deteriorating relationships, and turmoil, and with no visible successes, failure follows. So although under crisis conditions followers may be tolerant of leadership behaviors they would not otherwise support, there are limits to how much slack the leader will be afforded. These limits are correlated with the background of the leader, and are influenced by whether or not, or how quickly, things are seen as improving.

As the situation is seen as more benign, or even comfortable, and the appropriate changes are less obvious, or the culture more confident it has weathered problems before and can do so again, outside leaders may find that simply insisting upon compliance can create significant resistance and resentment. In such situations, the effects of charisma and reputation may be short-lived. Unless benefits to the organization and to followers become apparent quickly, only savvy change leadership will yield consistently positive results. These are the times when real leadership consists of leading followers through the process of self-discovery—asking them to help identify the problems and, with guidance, having them develop strategies for fixing them.

We earlier mentioned Carly Fiorina's problems at Hewlett-Packard. As an outsider, she had little to rely on by way of personal credibility with followers. Unlike in the situation at Nissan, HP employees did not really feel things were all that broken, and their proud tradition suggested they knew what to do and had a unique cultural advantage in doing it their own way. Relying mostly on charisma, or personal swagger, Fiorina envisioned changes that, in the long run, may have been appropriate. Lacking change savvy, she failed to persuade enough people to embrace the changes, and, obviously, using only positional power was not enough to carry the day. Charisma and demands for compliance just didn't do it!

Home Depot's Bob Nardelli, also an outsider, was chosen for his reputation as a master of operations at General Electric. To many observers, his focus on operations, cost-cutting, and improved controls were the very things the company needed following the heady growth overseen by its founders—a perception not necessarily shared by most employees. Applying his expertise, and relying mostly on positional power (creating an environment that has been described by some as a "culture of fear"[6]), in a setting where the "crisis" was not widely perceived, Nardelli encountered major disappointments.

In fact, the proud culture characterized as "bleeding orange" and priding itself on its service orientation resented operational improvements that had a negative impact on customer service, such as reducing inventory and staffing levels in the stores, and bristled at the new leader's attacks on their business acumen, exemplified by the quote attributed to him earlier. For years, in spite of many changes that lifted revenues and profits, the stock price languished, a mass exodus of senior people took place, morale kept sinking, customer service suffered, investor relations went sour, and everyone's impatience grew, leading to Nardelli's ouster.

When urgency is not widely perceived, and the culture is strong, outside leaders absolutely need to engage in change-savvy behaviors if they are to succeed—reputation and positional power just won't do it! Even when urgency is widely perceived, change leaders still need to convince followers that they understand the situation and can formulate and implement changes that will help fix the situation. It is interesting to note that of these seven "outsiders," five entered a situation widely recognized as broken and in need of repair (Nissan, NYPD, IBM, Xerox, and Avon), and thus may have been given the benefit of the doubt to see if they could fix things.

Four of these leaders increased their influence as they began to make a difference, and ultimately succeeded. Ghosn (at Nissan) relied mostly on compliance demands, but had healthy doses of inspiration and reputation to back him up. Bratton at the NYPD quickly gained some victories in the form of falling crime statistics and increased his credibility by fighting for police resources. Gerstner at IBM and Jung at Avon, lacking substantial reputation reservoirs relevant to the businesses they took over, relied more on persuasion through savvy change management and also succeeded. However, even when a crisis exists, our example of an outsider who failed (Thoman at Xerox) suggests that the absence of charisma or relevant reputation, coupled with a lack of change savvy and an overreliance on position power, leads to disaster. Such leaders take followers from skepticism to cynicism to open rebellion, precipitating further crisis. Thoman saw his influence diminish as relationships soured and changes made things worse instead of better.

Under more benign circumstances, the two outsiders who did not enjoy success (Fiorina at HP and Nardelli at HD) came into strong cultures that did not necessarily agree things were broken and had trouble achieving small victories as a means of gaining influence (in fact, Fiorina was busy crafting her grand strategy of merging with another company), and while one had charisma (Fiorina) and the other had a strong reputation (Nardelli), these were not enough to carry the day. Change savvy, which neither possessed in great measure, is important when an outsider enters an organization not widely perceived to be "broken." It becomes even more so when the culture is strong.

THE INSIDER AS CHANGE LEADER

Having looked at seven outsiders, let us look at some insiders charged with driving change in their organizations. Let's consider Anne Mulcahy at Xerox (who replaced Thoman). She was an insider, having spent twenty-four years with the company and been promoted to CEO from heading human resources (HR). Although HR is not usually considered the most fertile ground for growing future CEOs for technology companies, it is a position associated with some knowledge about people and change. Under Mulcahy's leadership, Xerox has regained its market leadership in high-end copying machines, cut its debt, settled charges with the SEC, cut overhead, and increased profits in each of the past four years. She may be on her way to one of the most significant rescues in corporate history.

How did she do it? Although she enjoyed interpersonal credibility with key individuals and a good reputation based on her earlier jobs in the company, she did it mostly through the display of change savvy. Asked about how she channeled her efforts early on in the turnaround, she remembers advice she received from Warren Buffett: "You'd better take care of your customers and employees as if your life depended on it." She goes on to say, "It would be like winning the battle and losing the war if you end up with a bunch of happy people on Wall Street . . . but your customers and employees don't really feel that sense of commitment and loyalty from the company."[7] Strength of relationships only available to the insider plus change savvy carried the day.

Another insider, Jamie Dimon, CEO of J.P. Morgan Chase, left Citigroup to lead Banc One, where he engineered a turnaround. He came to J.P. Morgan Chase when it acquired Banc One, first becoming president and then CEO. Known as brash, loud, unruly, even rude, and not above using intimidation and fear as motivators, he nevertheless had other reservoirs of goodwill to draw on that helped with driving change.

First, the sheer passion and intensity he brought to his job (charisma), as well as the reputation for success he brought with him from the job he did at Banc One, were motivators. Furthermore, in spite of his yelling and intimidation, he forged a bond with many followers—a bond based on trust, shared values, and mutual gain (credibility)—not to mention that he's made many followers rich. *Fortune* magazine quotes one of his subordinates as saying, "He can be a total pain, over demanding, but you'd trust your life to him."[8] Again, strength of relationships, building trust, reputation for success, and then delivering results have all made for successful changes led by an insider.

However, not all insiders have an edge. Some may have gotten where they are through operational successes, without having built the relationships that would later allow them to influence people to support their changes. Or they were so change-challenged (the opposite of change savvy) that they drained whatever was left in their relationship, reputation, or charisma reservoirs, being left with no leverage.

Earlier we mentioned Jacques Nasser and his short term as Ford CEO. Nasser was an insider, working his way up the organization and gaining a reputation as a turnaround expert; like Ghosn at Renault, he even earned the label "Jac the Knife."

Unfortunately, Nasser displayed very little change savvy as CEO, quickly depleting the reservoirs he had filled in his previous positions. Like Thoman at Xerox, he had no sense of the impact his many changes were having, he was not well-enough connected to his people to get realistic feedback, and he managed to alienate every important constituency, from employees to dealers to suppliers to the union and even to the Ford family. Taken one at a time, many of his strategic initiatives had a great deal of merit. He understood the business very well. However, he did not understand the process of change well enough to create a credible set of change initiatives and properly coordinate them.

Finally, let us look at another "insider," Durk Jager at Procter & Gamble (P&G). Jager, though he had risen through the ranks, did so mostly in Europe, developing a disdain for the corporate culture, seeing it as insular and as a barrier to change and growth. Those in the know understood that major changes were necessary. The company seemed to lack a strategy beyond cost-cutting; innovation and growth were stalling. Jager, upon being named CEO, immediately embarked on a series of tumultuous changes. Unfortunately, his approach to implementation reflected his disdain for the culture, alienating almost everyone. He was forced to resign. "Instead of pushing P&G to excel . . . the torrent of proclamations and initiatives during Jager's 17-month reign nearly brought the venerable company to a grinding halt."[9]

From our examination of these four insiders, it should be pretty obvious that positional power alone will not achieve results even if the leader is intimately familiar with the company and its business. Relationships are important for getting things done, and being change savvy is a powerful complement to relationships. Being oblivious to change issues will quickly sabotage even good change ideas, even under crisis conditions, *unless the leader achieves some quick successes that bolster trust in his or her ability to lead the way out of the crisis.*

There is a limit to what people will take from a bully change leader without offsetting benefits. Interestingly, it is the theme of "too much too fast" that seems to be the undoing of many leaders because it keeps them from enjoying the fruits of incremental successes that would fill their reputation, relationship, and change savvy reservoirs. We will return to this theme in a later chapter.

IS THERE A PATTERN HERE?

Having argued for the relative potency of our different reservoirs of influence and provided illustrations of eleven change leaders, what can we conclude? Credibility through personal relationships, existing ones or those based on change savvy, is the most effective tool for change leaders (Gerstner, Jung, Dimon, Mulcahy). Charisma, or reputation alone, rarely work (Fiorina, Nardelli) unless there is a widely perceived crisis and the leader's reputation gets validated fairly quickly by visible improvements (Ghosn, Bratton). Positional power alone will almost always yield failure, especially absent change savvy (Thoman, Nasser, Jager). Most important, charisma, reputation, and coercion wear thin unless followers see the benefits of the change initiative. The mantra of "no pain, no gain" holds little allure when the pain is obvious and ongoing but the gain seems elusive or continues to accrue to others.

It is best to think of reservoirs as expendable resources, with not all of them being necessarily, or easily, renewable. The goodwill associated with strong relationships and savvy change leadership will be depleted to the degree leaders do not deliver the promised outcomes, or do so at a cost deemed unacceptably high by followers. These reservoirs are replenished, and their levels increased, as leadership behaviors are seen as instrumental in improving organizational and individual well-being. Similarly, the reputation reservoir gets replenished as leaders validate these perceptions through their actions, but it can also be quickly depleted if not accompanied by change-savvy behaviors.

The charisma reservoir, besides being depleted when not accompanied by savvy change leadership that gets results, may also evaporate if the leader begins to appeal to values not shared by followers. For example, a leader who energized employees by rallying them around a "made in the USA" emotion will suffer an erosion of support if she later uses her charisma to promote change that includes the outsourcing of work to another country. Similarly, the charismatic leader in a medical or pharmaceutical setting who appealed to followers on the basis of shared values of putting patients first and doing no harm could run into trouble if he advocates cost-cutting or other changes viewed as harmful to patients.

Most people do not possess great amounts of coercive power, or are not willing to use it freely, nor are they blessed with charismatic personalities. Most operate in settings where their past behaviors are relatively well known, such that their relationships and reputations, such as they are, are established. Where should leaders focus when it comes to leading change? They should focus on establishing trusting relationships in general and on improving their change-specific skills in particular. Strong leader-follower relationships, in general, will take some of the pressure off of leaders when leading change, whereas improvements in their approaches to change leadership will further strengthen such relationships over time as well as bolster their reputations as change leaders.

If leaders find themselves new to the setting, or having been brought in as part of the change, careful attention to change leadership is the surest way to start forming relationships and establish credibility as a change leader. Though power, charisma, and a good reputation will certainly help get them get started with change, and may even help achieve some short-term successes, these are not substitutes for leader-follower relationships carefully nurtured and personal credibility appropriately earned and applied.

Over and over again, savvy leaders note how, when they first came into a new setting, they kept their ear to the ground and focused on learning about the business and the situation. When Patricia Woertz was named CEO of Archer Daniels Midland, the food and ethanol giant, one insider commented, "Bringing an outsider, a woman no less, into a company that's a bastion of lifers and good ol' boys—I can't tell you how huge a change that is." What did she do upon arrival? "My objectives in the first 100 days have been to listen and learn and build trust. I've met with over 4,000 employees, been to 32 ADM locations. I want to get to a lot of people early on and find out what we do very well and where we can improve." Did it work? "I tell people you only get one chance to make a first impression," says Steven Mills, ADM's controller, "and Pat made a great one."[10]

CONCLUSION

As we noted in the previous chapter, leaders need to understand where their influence comes from. Here we emphasized the need to read the situation and decipher the implications, limitations, or advantages associated with sources of influence given the situation. Different influence reservoirs can be used in various ways depending on the situations facing leaders.

No matter how much positional power leaders enjoy, how sound their reputations, and how good their change ideas, success may still be elusive if they can't build the kinds of relationships that make those being led want to follow. Leaders who succeed with major changes bring credibility based on ongoing, insider relationships, or, if outsiders, they tread carefully, listen, learn, build up credits, and try to create smaller, quick wins.

Organizations that feel compelled to bring in outsiders when change is necessary need to carefully weigh why they're doing so. Have they thought about the disadvantage an outsider may have over a competent insider? If you are the outsider who is brought in, what advantages or disadvantages do you bring with you, and what role should the urgency of the situation play in your choice of leadership behaviors? In our opening quote from Maureen Chiquet, the CEO of Chanel, she recognized the need to go slow and listen. She came from a mass merchandiser, The Gap, and became an American heading one of France's most prestigious design houses. To learn the business, understand the culture, gain acceptance, and not reinforce any stereotypes the French may have had about Americans and American managers, she "taped" her mouth and opened her ears.

As Pfeffer and Sutton note in their book *Hard Facts, Dangerous Half-Truths and Total Nonsense*,[11] the notion that leaders are able to come in and quickly make a big, positive difference needs some debunking. It is very difficult to come in from the outside and drive major changes. We need to understand that successful leaders from the outside such as Gerstner, Jung, and Woertz, if they don't have industry experience, take their time to learn and, in the process, build relationships and credibility. Those that do have industry experience may be able to short-circuit some of this learning. Those who are lacking change savvy often fail.

Yet the churning of executives between corporations, especially at the highest levels, suggests that we haven't quite figured this out. Organizations still look for the quick shakeup, they still envy what someone has done elsewhere and want him or her to replicate it here (preferably in a very short period of time), they still look for functional and business expertise instead of change expertise—yet they say they want change!

Though the events surrounding high-level executives are far more public and open to scrutiny and interpretation, it is important to note that everything we've said in the past two chapters, the role of different influence reservoirs, the limitations of being an outsider, or the role played by crises, all apply to managers everywhere in the organization. The mental calculus should be the same for leaders at all levels of organizations as they assess their sources of influence and the situation they face in plotting an approach to change. As we see from many of these examples, poor change leadership can be devastating to companies. In contrast, the competent change leader is worth his or her weight in gold.

6

PEOPLE'S MOTIVATION TO CHANGE

"When I was a mechanic, I knew how much faster I could fix an airplane when I wanted to fix it than when I didn't. I've tried to make it so our guys want to do it."
Gordon Bethune, CEO who engineered a major turnaround at Continental Airlines[1]

In previous chapters, we discussed the role of the change leader in motivating followers to support the change effort. Continuing with our focus on WHO, this and the next chapter will examine the role of followers. Specifically, we will address two important but mostly overlooked issues affecting followers' behavior—their motivation to change and their capacity for change. Ultimately, performance is a function of what people can do and how motivated they are to do it.

FOLLOWERS' PERSPECTIVE

There is no such thing as "organizational change"! (Seems like a strange assertion for a book on the topic of organizational change, doesn't it?) For the most part, organizations no more change than they think, feel, perceive, have attitudes, or express opinions. When we say an organization has made the transition from "point A" to "point B," we really mean many individuals within the organization have changed their behavior, such that, collectively, the organization now reflects these changes, giving rise to the observation "the organization has changed."

Although this point may seem obvious, much of what has been written about organizational change, as we've already noted, focuses on managing the change process (the HOW of change). Most treatments of change management assume that if we simply follow common change management prescriptions, in other words, handle change "correctly" by communicating effectively, allowing for employee input, creating a sense of urgency, and so on, employees will follow and respond in the desired ways, and the change will be successful.

Unfortunately, it is not this simple. We all know that getting people to change their behavior is often a major challenge, and sometimes seems almost impossible. Not only are people at the core of successful organizational change, they also represent the greatest challenge to our mastery of change. Structures, systems, processes, strategies—these are relatively simple to understand and even fix; people are not. As is often said, the "soft" issues are the hard ones. Employees come in all shapes and sizes; have different backgrounds, different skills and abilities, different personalities, different dispositions, different hang-ups, and different motivations and aspirations, all of which affect their actions. Yet when planning change, leaders often don't take these differences into account.

One reason why leaders tend to ignore the complexities of human responses to change is that incorporating the role of individuals into their thinking about change and allowing for differences among individuals further complicate an already very complex issue. Thus individuals in organizations are often relegated to the role of impediments on the path to goals, rather than as the keys to achieving these goals. Many leaders develop a fatalistic attitude toward the role of people in change, giving up trying to manage it and, worse, denying personal responsibility for how individuals may respond. Over and over again, when change is going poorly or evidence exists that performance and morale are in the dumps during a change, leaders challenged with such evidence respond with refrains such as "It's not me, it's them," "They just don't get it," "I can't understand it," or "I wish they'd get with the program."

As an example, when the director of the Centers for Disease Control and Prevention (CDC) was grilled by the chair of a Congressional oversight committee concerning evidence of serious defections of scientific talent and low morale in her agency following a series of major changes, she gave "assurances that it was normal for employees to be anxious about change."[2] As things continued to deteriorate, the director again repeated, "I don't know any organization that's gone through significant change where morale hasn't been an issue."[3] In her e-mail to employees in response to negative press coverage in the

CDC's hometown, Atlanta, she noted that the substance of the controversies was not really important, but they "represent symptoms of a disease within CDC. Frankly, I believe it is a chronic (or perhaps autoimmune) disease that pre-dates our leadership, but there is strong evidence of an acute exacerbation. . . . We must diagnose this disease. . . . We must also treat this disease. It will require intensive care, but not radical surgery. . . . Convalescence will be slow, but full recovery is possible."[4]

What an interesting use of medical metaphors. "They" are sick and "we" (leadership) must heal them (and are not really responsible for the condition). To continue with the epidemiological metaphors, shouldn't the organization charged with the study of infectious diseases, when confronted with an epidemic of low morale and high turnover among its most valued employees, be more diligent in seeking out and eradicating the sources of the infection? Shouldn't it address the factors that promote its spread? In other words, what were employees exposed to that made them sick? How does the organization deal with the source of the "infection"? Now that employees are "sick," even if they are "convalescing," how do the change plans need to be adjusted to that reality?

Becoming defensive about failures to anticipate and deal with such issues, people go on the offensive and place the burden on the targets of change—this is where "if you can't stand the heat get out of the kitchen" comes in. Perhaps they even purchase bulk quantities of *Who Moved My Cheese?* and distribute the book to employees as a sort of self-help manual for dealing with constant change, whether it is well-thought-out and implemented or not.

Instead, leaders should be asking questions such as What determines employees' willingness to change and how can we influence it? What do we know about employees' capacity for dealing with the change and how should it affect our approach? What might be the anticipated emotional and attitudinal reactions to the change? Do we expect different responses on the part of different people, and if so, how can we use that in our planning? Leaders often gloss over such issues, yet it is human behavior, in support, in opposition, or in passive resistance, that ultimately will drive the success of changes. The materials in this and the next chapter are aimed at helping leaders think these issues through.

THE DECISION TO EXERT EFFORT
ON BEHALF OF A CHANGE

In previous chapters, we discussed ways in which leaders can influence followers' behaviors. However, followers' behaviors are not just influenced by what
the leader does; they are also a function of various follower characteristics. A
person's decision to exert effort, such as in support of a change, can be boiled
down to three questions:

1. Can I do it if I try?
2. What will happen if I succeed (or fail)?
3. How much do I value such consequences?

The first two questions may be thought of as probabilistic assessments, in
other words, the likelihood of being able to perform at a particular level, and
the likelihood of certain outcomes being associated with that performance
level. The last question is an assessment of the attractiveness (or unattractive-
ness) of the anticipated outcomes.

Using this formulation, motivation is thought to be highest when the individual is confident of being able to attain the desired performance and expects
valued outcomes to then follow. Motivation is thought to decrease to the extent there is slippage in any of these factors. That is, if individuals do not think
they can attain the requisite performance level, it does not matter what they
associate with successful performance, or how much they value these outcomes. Similarly, if the individual does not value the associated outcomes, or
does not believe they are likely to follow from successful performance, motivation will decrease even if the individual is confident of being able to perform
at the requisite level.

Obviously, this is a simplified representation of a very complex cognitive
process.[5] The real value of this perspective of followers' motivation is not in
trying to quantify what may be unquantifiable, subjective assessments. Rather,
its value is as a guide for directing leaders' thinking about those they are leading through change and deciding what they as change leaders can or cannot
influence, and how much.

WHAT FACTORS INFLUENCE THE
ANSWERS TO THESE QUESTIONS?

Let's examine the first question—"Can I do it if I try?" At the individual level, *personal characteristics* such as skills, abilities, experience, or physical attributes and other demographics may affect one's belief that he or she can achieve the desired behaviors. What we commonly refer to as personality (for example, self-esteem), and other internal states (such as needs, motives, fears) may also shape this assessment.

However, the behavior of *leaders* also influences this assessment. The previously discussed personal credibility ascribed to a leader is anchored in the history of productive encounters with that leader, with these shaping estimates of future encounters (for example, she was right about me being able to handle the last change so maybe she'll be right again); change-savvy leaders are expected to provide the support necessary for change, thus making success more likely; and leaders' charisma and reputation may shape individuals' assessments of their own prospects (for example, may inspire self-confidence). Similarly, the *context* may also shape this assessment. Whether the organization has previously provided resources, support, and training as opposed to asking people to make do without will also influence individuals' answer to this question.

The second question—"What will happen if I succeed (or fail)?"—is also subject to personal, leadership, and organizational influences. Personality characteristics such as optimism and other dispositions such as flexibility, future orientation, or anxiety will shape people's assessments of the consequences associated with successfully implementing their portion of the change. We've all seen negative, cynical, or fatalistic reactions such as "Where does it get you?" "Yeah, right, that's what they said last time!" or "I'll believe it when I see it" on the part of people who undoubtedly *could* do something, but were not enthusiastic about doing it.

To the degree that change leaders can persuade followers that goal attainment will be rewarded, they can influence followers' motivational calculus. This is where our leadership discussion of persuasion and influence, as opposed to coercion, again comes in. Credible leaders are trusted to follow through on recognition and rewards associated with both personal and change goal attainment and to celebrate individual and team accomplishments. Organizations can also have an impact on this assessment by their processes and systems that link outcomes to performance rather than to favoritism, political connection, or other, capricious criteria.

The third question—"How much do I value such consequences?"—is far less open to leadership and organizational influences, as it reflects personal values. Financial rewards will not be motivating to the degree that the individual does not value monetary outcomes, and promises of advancement opportunities are not as motivating for those low in achievement orientation or those who have other interests in life into which they pour their energy.

However, even for this question, leaders are not without influence opportunities. Followers will place a greater value on rewards from leaders with whom they want to maintain a positive relationship, from leaders seen as influential, or from leaders whose goals they share. Just think of how you feel when someone you admire recognizes your efforts. The same is definitely not true for people above you for whom you have little or no regard. Similarly, the value of a given reward may be influenced by the context in which it is provided. For instance, in some organizations, a particular type of office may mean a great deal, whereas in a different organization no importance would be put on the exact same office space.

In Figure 6.1 we illustrate this sequence of questions thought to shape followers' motivation to exert energy on behalf of a change and the relative contributions of the follower, the leader, and the organizational context at each step. The thickness of the arrows is intended to reflect relative potency; in other words, although follower characteristics may be most important in influencing the first and last components of this sequence, leaders and organizations have the greatest influence on the middle component.

We can now see that leaders' influence reservoirs (compliance, personal credibility, change savvy, charisma, and reputation) may be thought of as operating through this motivational model. As we noted earlier, personal credibility, change savvy, and even charisma can all be used to increase followers' self-confidence that they can engage in the requisite behaviors. Credible and change-savvy leaders may also be more trusted by followers to deliver promised outcomes upon successful attainment of the new behaviors, and rewards

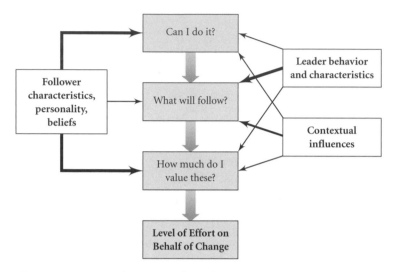

Figure 6.1. Factors shaping employees' motivation to change

from certain leaders, such as approval, may be more valued than the same rewards from leaders not possessing these influence mechanisms.

Similarly, the organizational context can also influence each of the three components of the motivational model, but probably to a lesser degree than the leader can. Finally, characteristics of the followers play a major role in influencing the "can I do it" and "how much do I value it" aspects of the model, leaving leaders with a significant "unknown" to be diagnosed when trying to understand why people do what they do when called upon to support change.

DIFFERENT STROKES FOR DIFFERENT FOLKS

Earlier we noted that personal characteristics play a part in how different individuals may answer each of the three questions (Can I do it if I try? What will happen if I succeed or fail? How much do I value such consequences?). Because individuals differ from each other in many ways, what can change leaders do? First, they need to work at understanding that they may very well run into such differences—when it comes to change, one size does not fit all. Second, to the extent they are aware of such personal differences, they need to incorporate them into their diagnoses of change situations. Third, and just as important, they need to be careful about letting stereotypes about people unduly influence their thinking, especially if such stereotypes are more myth than reality.

Although a full exploration of how individuals can differ is far beyond the scope of this book, our purpose for dealing with them here is to demonstrate that such differences might affect change-related behaviors. We also want to illustrate some of what is known about such differences, from our own and others' research.

Demographics

Most of what people think about in terms of demographics (such as age and sex) and their relationship to change-related behaviors falls under the heading of "conventional wisdoms," such as "older people resist change." We have conducted research across hundreds of changes and thousands of people and have found *no evidence* for any *consistent* relationship between age and reactions to change. Nor have we found differences in reactions to change based on sex, job tenure, or organizational tenure. Once again, simplistic notions or "truisms" tend not to hold up. Demographics do not appear to be good predictors of responses to change, though because of their obviousness, it certainly would be convenient if they were.

This is not saying that we might not find an organization in which older or longer-tenured members (or any other group) are more or less supportive of change. This could be because they were recruited differently, socialized differently, or had different experiences with past change in the organization. Furthermore, there may be certain situations in which demographics play an important role (for example, younger work populations may have an easier time adopting text-messaging technologies at work). The point we are making is that on average, and across many different types of settings, these demographics don't seem to explain much in the way of people's reactions to change. As such, we need to be cautious about making generalizations. When it comes to change, stereotypes, especially related to sex or age, can be misleading.

Personality Differences

Unlike with demographics, the search for personality determinants of change-related behaviors yields a different picture. The most significant personality variable that has been shown by past research to be related to performance in organizations is *conscientiousness.*[6] This factor, besides the everyday meaning of the term, captures peoples' predisposition to be achievement-oriented, along with their desire to be consistent and reliable. Our own research has also found this personality factor to be important in understanding employees' change-related responses.

As the label suggests, conscientious people are concerned with living up to their own standards of achievement and reliability. We have found that they can respond negatively to change situations that make achieving their goals more difficult. In contrast, they seem to respond very positively when appropriate levels of support are provided during change so that they can continue to perform well.[7]

We may extrapolate from this that changes which disrupt day-to-day routines and threaten the maintenance of performance standards will be greeted negatively by highly conscientious people unless steps are taken to facilitate the transition. In other words, leaders need to provide the appropriate support that enables conscientious individuals to maintain their personal performance standards. People who are less conscientious may not be so concerned, taking more of an "I don't really care" attitude. In fact, we've found that less conscientious employees responded to change about the same regardless of their leader's support or facilitation.

Another personality dimension that may be important in shaping people's responses to change, especially disruptive or anxiety-inducing change, is called *emotional stability.* In essence, emotional stability reflects the absence of anxiety or the ability to remain calm under stressful conditions, such as during times of change. We have found that people low in emotional stability performed less well during change even when they possessed high levels of ability.[8]

Furthermore, when their job was significantly affected by the change, people with low emotional stability felt far more negatively about how the change was handled than those with high emotional stability. When changes had minimal impact on people's jobs, emotional stability was not related to change reactions. Because a significant impact on people's day-to-day jobs or routines is related to the levels of stress they are likely to experience, and change may be stress-inducing in general, leaders need to be alert to how different people respond to stress situations. One important conclusion we can draw from this is that simply focusing on skill training, or being confident that people have the ability or skills to master a change, might miss the key point of why individuals are struggling with the change. In the case of personality factors, how people react to change may be a function of what they are rather than what they know.

So what is a leader to do with these results about personality differences? Certainly, we are not advocating that psychological workups or personality profiles be obtained for all employees. Instead, we want to illustrate our earlier theme, which is that leaders can't simply ignore the role played by individuals in their organizations if they want to have a better understanding of change reactions. Who the followers are can influence their response to change efforts. Therefore, if leaders seek to understand such differences, they may be better able to figure out how best to proceed with a particular change initiative. For instance, they can modify their change approaches to account for personality differences by working to assure their most conscientious people that they will help them remain productive through the change, or by attempting to reduce the anxiety associated with change for those they deem most vulnerable to such feelings.

Work Attitudes

Not only will relatively stable personal traits, such as those just discussed, influence reactions to change situations, but so will followers' attitudes. One attitude we have found to strongly influence followers' responses to change is how committed employees feel to the organization and its goals, often referred to as *organizational commitment*. In one recently completed large-scale study we found that those more committed to their organizations were more supportive of change efforts that were handled well, even when the leaders involved were not rated highly on general leadership.[9]

Those high in commitment were also supportive of changes led by strong, transformational leaders even when these leaders did not do such a good job with handling the specifics of the particular change. In other words, committed employees don't need an awful lot of convincing; they'll follow leaders during change who are savvy vis-à-vis the change at hand, or leaders with whom they have established longer-term bonds or relationships. This is consistent with our discussions of the different influence "buckets" in our leadership chapters. However, now we can further qualify these discussions by pointing out that the one-on-one relationship buckets, personal credibility and change savvy, will be especially effective in motivating organizationally committed employees to support a change.

Now we need to share the bad news. If employees report little or no commitment to the organization, then leadership does not have much of an effect on support for the change, whether the leader is seen as a good leader in general or as having done things well for the particular change. This helps explain why leaders often can become very frustrated when they feel they've done everything they can think of to handle the change well, but they still don't get support from some employees. This may be because these employees are negatively disposed toward the organization. There may be little leaders can do, in the short run, to get these employees fired up about the changes that need to be implemented. They will have to rely more on their more committed followers, and try to better align the goals of the less committed people with the goals of the organization in the hope of increasing their commitment to the new path. This is where short-term, less grandiose but mutually beneficial (to organization and to employees) changes come in.

These findings may also help explain why, when faced with strong time pressures to create change, and dealing with employees low in organizational commitment, leaders often resort to their positional power to try to push the changes through—often resulting in poor outcomes. Our model suggests that a thorough assessment of the change situation will help identify such barriers, causing the leader to reconsider some of the ambitious change plans, choosing instead to first alter the situation by strengthening the bonds between employees and the organization before proceeding with major changes.

Sometimes it doesn't take a lot to create a modest amount of goodwill for the organization, with such goodwill ultimately translating into support for change. As we have noted earlier, when Gerstner first took the reins at IBM, he listened to employees and initially proposed changes in areas in which most people agreed change was needed and that had been frustrating them—a "low-hanging fruit" strategy. In addition, the symbolic power of attending to employees, especially those who have not been heard in the past or may have felt more alienated from the organization, and making some good faith efforts to address a few of their concerns, should not be underestimated. In this way, a very different foundation can be established for future, more pervasive changes.

Finally, there is one more important finding from our study of organizational commitment and change, and it too falls under the "bad news" or caution for leaders heading. We noted that committed employees will respond well to leaders who either handle the change well or are viewed as good overall leaders. However, our data also show that when leaders are seen neither as good leaders, in general, nor as handling the change situation well, committed employees respond in the same manner as those who are far less committed—namely, not supportive of the change. In other words, committed employees expect their organizational leaders to do just that—lead. They can handle good leaders who fall down on a particular change; they can handle not-so-good leaders who are diligent about handling a particular change; they apparently can't handle low-credibility leaders who also bungle the change effort.

This may have been the combination of factors that led to the downfall of Bob Nardelli at Home Depot. Before his arrival, employees were positively disposed toward their organization, often said to "bleed orange." Nardelli came in, not particularly charismatic, lacking a retailing or home improvement reputation; his early encounters with employees did not suggest the beginnings of a strong bond based on personal credibility; and he definitely seemed to lack change management skills. When he met with resistance, he apparently got more and more frustrated, resorted to more and more reliance on positional power, surrounded himself more and more with people loyal to him (imported from the outside), all further stymieing his plans and creating public fallout. One would speculate that those most committed to the organization probably resisted the most.

Given the importance of organizational commitment for explaining people's reactions to change, a few words are warranted about its origins. Although a full discussion of the antecedents of organizational commitment is beyond the scope of this book, it is generally linked to employees' perceptions of how fairly they are treated and how strongly they identify with the organization's goals. One thing for us to consider is that the perception of fair treatment is based not only on the allocation of rewards, such as pay or promotion, but also on the general treatment of people in the organization.

Remember Warren Buffet's advice to Ann Mulcahy at Xerox to take care of her employees "as if her life depended on it?" Similarly, the founder of the Container Store, Kip Tindell, was recently quoted as saying "If you take care of your employees, they'll take care of the customers—and that will take care of your shareholders."[10] The founder of Costco, Jim Sinegal, expressed the same view when he said, "We want to . . . take care of our customers, take care of our people and respect our suppliers." He then added that if they were to do those things, "we're going to reward shareholders."[11]

Although we hear a great deal about organizations being "lean and mean," we cannot overemphasize the importance of fair treatment as a means of gaining commitment, with that commitment being a key ingredient in motivating people to embrace change that benefits the organization. As the preceding quotes suggest, there are plenty of smart leaders who have figured this out. Imposing repeated changes on people, with little time for adjustment, less-than-sufficient support, and less-than-equitable distribution of pain and benefits, often translates into feelings of unfair treatment. This, in turn, reduces commitment to the organization, and then these same companies wonder why employees "resist" change.

Going back to our discussion of the Finance and Accounting Department in the mergers example in Chapter 3, one very plausible explanation for the low level of organizational commitment reported by that department's employees may have been their experience of one change after another without appropriate organizational consideration for their mounting difficulties and distress. We will have more to say about the effects of frequent changes in Chapter 8.

Thus both our anecdotal and empirical data point to the downward spiral of poorly managed or too frequent change. These appear to cause a decline in organizational commitment, which, in turn, leads to deterioration in support for subsequent change. Under these circumstances, leaders then resort to a reliance on raw power as a motivator, which further decreases commitment, and so on. Instead, when at all possible, leaders would be wise to focus on repairing employee-organization relationships before proceeding with major changes.

CONCLUSION

We've introduced this discussion of followers' motivation to support change for two reasons. First, we need to move beyond broad generalizations or conventional wisdoms about people and change. Thus "all people resist change" will set the stage for said resistance. Having a framework for asking why people may respond in particular ways to change initiatives and what might be done about it should help leaders be more purposive and focused in their change leadership behaviors.

Second, working with this motivational framework allows leaders to examine motivation from multiple perspectives. Some changes are going to generate pretty similar motivational reactions on the part of most or all people. For example, when you ask an IT group to train their outsourcing replacements, when all they have to look forward to is losing their jobs, you should not be surprised if their motivation for carrying out this task is absent. Thus, at the general level, one can ask the following questions:

- Do people believe the goals of the change are achievable? If they do not, there are various potential causes to consider (for example, the goals may be too difficult; the time allotted is unrealistic; the approach, process, or support is inadequate; our track record with change is poor).

- What do people think will be the consequences associated with achieving the desired change? If by achieving the change goals the company will become more prosperous, but many people are likely to lose their jobs, that's a different calculus than the company becoming more prosperous and each person individually doing so as well.

- How are the various organizational and personal outcomes valued (going from highly negative to highly positive and somehow balanced, or netted-out in one's mind)? On balance, do individuals believe they'll be better off if the change succeeds?

In contrast, some changes may have different motivational impacts on different individuals within the organization or within our group. Leaders may focus on such individuals either because they have reason to believe these individuals may represent special cases, or because they are critical to the change effort, or because the leaders are puzzled by the individuals' change-related responses.

Changes that are threatening or burdensome to some may not be so to others. Changes that are inherently stressful will have different effects on people depending on their general anxiety levels. Using such knowledge, leaders can either alter their change implementation approach (for example, target the conscientious and emotionally stable people first, hoping that this will reduce anxiety for others as they see the change unfold) or be more alert to different reactions on the part of different people (for example, check for stress reactions, negative attitudes, or expressed dissatisfaction on the part of otherwise valued performers).

Thus leaders should be asking, What can I do to increase the perceived likelihood that a given individual, team, or the whole organization will succeed with the change? What can I do to increase the perceived linkage between working hard on behalf of the change and realizing personally valued outcomes? What can the organization do to remove barriers so that people feel the change is achievable? What can the organization do to cement the relationship between successful change efforts and personally valued outcomes? What can I or the organization do to select, develop, or train people that will better help them deal with change situations?

Even more important, leaders need to understand that in the eyes of organizational members, changes are not independent events. Each change, how it was handled, how it turned out, and what it extracted from individuals forms beliefs about future changes. Such beliefs then shape future change-related behaviors. When we say people are cynical about change, they didn't become so overnight.

7

PEOPLE'S CAPACITY FOR CHANGE

"As Woods slipped . . . an insidious thought crossed the game's collective mind: Is the Tiger Era over? So cataclysmic seemed the struggle that theorists looked for causes in life issues: marriage, his father's health, burnout, injury, even ennui . . . he gradually acknowledged the process of a swing change. . . . "
Golf Digest[1]

In the previous chapter we tackled people's motivation to embrace or work on behalf of a given change. But what if the person wants to attain the desired new performance but cannot? Human performance is determined by motivation *and* capacity or ability. In this chapter, the final in our treatment of the critical WHO issues, we will explore the question of capacity to change.

What determines an individual's capacity to attain the behaviors required or dictated by an organizational change? First, there is the question of whether the person possesses the knowledge or abilities to perform at the new level. However, another important consideration is whether the person has the capacity or energy (psychological, physiological, and emotional) to adapt to the new requirements. The first, the knowledge and abilities to perform the newly required behaviors, is rather obvious, receives a great deal of attention in many cases, and yet is still often overlooked or mismanaged.

For example, many a change initiative is accompanied by massive amounts of training. This is in recognition that the new behaviors will require new knowledge, skills, or both. However, there may still be questions about the amount, content, delivery, modality, and timing of the training; how well the training transfers to the work setting; and how prepared trainees are to benefit from the training.

Conversely, many organizations have made major changes that should have been accompanied by skill-building, but weren't. Companies have reorganized their salesforces from product orientation to geographical divisions, failing to adequately cross-train salespeople in the wider variety of product knowledge they would need to possess. Similarly, many companies have launched head-long into team-based initiatives, yet the basic team-related skills were not provided, frustrating team members who had no sense of how to run a meeting or how to deal with group dynamics.

Except in cases in which the need for new skills is obvious, by and large, in most organizational settings, the assumption is made that incumbents can master the new behaviors if only they want to. What's more, the assumption seems to be that they can do so more or less instantaneously. Such an assumption may or may not be valid, and any consideration of the WHO component of our model should include an examination of how people adapt to new requirements through the acquisition of new routines and the learning of new behaviors. This question is relevant for all changes, and may be the most overlooked aspect of the broader question of how people will respond to modifications in their work routines.

HOW DO PEOPLE ADAPT TO NEW CONDITIONS?

When conducting change workshops and seminars for managers, we often begin by asking the attendees for a show of hands of those participating in a variety of sports—golf, tennis, jogging, and so on. Using golf as an example, we ask the group a series of questions about a hypothetical, avid golfer. We begin by asking what would happen if said golfer saw a commercial for a new golf club that was technically so advanced that it "guaranteed" balls would go further, straighter, and with better control. Most people in the audience agree that our hypothetical golfer would want one.

We then ask them to assume that after forking over a rather tidy sum of money, the golfer receives the new club on Friday afternoon. On Saturday morning our golfer eagerly goes out for the first outing with the new club. We ask the group what they think the likely outcome will be of this first round of golf using the new club. Most people agree our golfer's score is likely to deteriorate when first switching to the new club. From this observation, and the subsequent discourse, we generate a variety of important points that can shape our thinking as change leaders.

Why did performance decline? Because whenever we make a significant change in our routine, a period of adjustment will follow. Our golfer has to incorporate the characteristics of the new club into his or her stance, grip, and swing and make appropriate adjustments. When we ask the group to name this phenomenon, they invariably refer to a *learning curve,* and agree this phenomenon applies to the acquisition of any new routine, in sports or at work.

What does our golfer say upon returning home from the disappointing outing and being confronted with the question, "How did it go, honey"? Most managers we run into seem to think the golfer would tell a "white lie" or, at least, sugarcoat the poor performance. When asked why this would be the case, managers offer a variety of explanations, including the need to justify the high cost of the club, possible embarrassment, and a general optimism that the new club represents a good investment and, with time, things will improve.

How long will it take for the golfer to achieve the hoped-for results? It depends on the golfer and on the club, they tell us. Skills, perseverance, and opportunities for practice will all create variations in performance levels. However, it is possible the club is not all that it's cracked up to be, or our golfer is not sufficiently skilled to take advantage of it, and hence performance may not improve beyond past performance, or may even decline.

The insights from such a discussion can be graphically represented, as we have done in Figures 7.1 and 7.2. In Figure 7.1, we plot the mythical line corresponding to the instantaneous and significant improvement hoped for upon the introduction of the change (the "myth"). In Figure 7.2, we introduce the change (new golf club), plot the subsequent decline in actual performance due to learning curve effects (shown in terms of the depth and duration of sub-par performance), and the more realistic expectation that performance will, all things being equal and after adjustment, improve to expected levels. Of course, it's possible, for a variety of reasons, for performance not even to attain pre-change levels.

Having discussed these various possibilities, we go back to the "learning curve" effect on performance depicted in Figure 7.2, and discuss its two major attributes—the depth of the decline and the duration of the recovery, or slope of the improvement curve. What could we as leaders do to mitigate the sudden fall-off in our golfer's performance? Among other things, we could have the

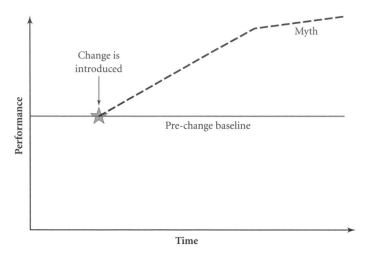

Figure 7.1. The myth of post-change performance

golfer practice before the first round, we could intensify training after the initial round, or we could provide coaching to go along with the initial and subsequent attempts to use the club.

What factors influence the slope of the learning curve? Factors include the skills of the golfer, the amount of time and effort (motivation) devoted to practice, assistance or support provided by others, other activities that may detract from the time or energy available for this task, and how good the new club really is. By now, it should be obvious that all of these insights about our golfer have organizational analogues.

If we substitute "enterprise software," "new technology," or "reorganization," for "new golf club," we see that the same processes operate, and may even be more potent, in an organization. Change is introduced, often at great expense, and immediate results are promised. Actual performance after the change is often below expectations, and those in charge are in denial, or embarrassed, and report the change is working about as expected. Eventually they may get it right, but usually with lower benefits and at greater cost than originally planned, or the change may fail so badly that they pull the plug on it altogether.

Having drawn a link between the golfer and organizational change realities, we can now elaborate on the organizational dynamics that can exacerbate or ameliorate these effects. For example, strict ROI (return on investment) requirements will increase the likelihood that the instantaneous improvement will be promised, or key cost factors ignored. This exaggeration of the cost-return ratio may improve the odds of receiving the go ahead for the change. Similarly, unrealistic expectations communicated or demanded by senior leadership may drive change leaders to agree to unrealistic schedules and milestones. Wanting to "fix" things quickly is an all too common pressure.

Along with business-related pressures to create unrealistic change expectations, there is also a natural tendency for changes or improvements to appear easier from what has been called the "observer" perspective,[2] typically of those who dictate or plan change rather than having to implement it. This is why, when we watch sporting events, it is common for us nonplayers to be unforgiving of the play of real players. From the comfort of the stands or our chairs in front of the TV, a play looks much less challenging than it does from field level ("He should have caught that ball" or "That was an easy out"). This phenomenon is consistent with our data, reported in Chapter 4, that leaders report experiencing lower levels of stress associated with a given change than do their followers.

However, we don't just have unrealistic expectations for others; we also minimize the difficulty of things we set out to do ourselves. How often have we

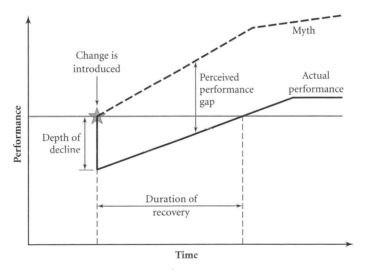

Figure 7.2. The reality of post-change performance

had "great" plans for a project, whether to clean the garage on the weekend or take on a home-improvement project, only to find that the task took much more time than anticipated, it was more complicated than we anticipated, or unexpected events derailed our good intentions? When we add together how easy things can look from a distance (the observer position) and how difficult it is both to gauge the requirements of new tasks and to foresee future, intervening events, it is not surprising a lot of changes end up being held to totally unrealistic expectations.

Clearly, excellent training and good change management practices will mitigate the depth and duration of the performance dip, because they begin to address a lot of the issues we have identified. Having skilled people, or people possessing some of the personal characteristics we described in the last chapter (those who are conscientious, emotionally stable, and so on), will speed up adaptation. Change leadership that is supportive, provides appropriate and timely resources, and controls environmental distractions may also speed up adaptation. However, the notion that performance immediately after a change will improve is, largely, a myth.

THE CONSEQUENCES OF LIVING THE CHANGE MYTH

Next, we ask leaders to reflect on the consequences of setting expectations along the lines of the "myth" and delivering along the line of the actual learning curve. The discussion now shifts to why performance that is perfectly reasonable by "reality" standards will be perceived as substandard by "mythical" standards. The perceived performance gap (in Figure 7.2) between these two curves, at any point in time, represents the possibility that satisfactory change progress, in other words, progress conforming to the learning curve, will, in fact, be viewed as unsatisfactory. This may precipitate a variety of "remedial" actions that may be unnecessary at best or counterproductive at worst.

For example, the change leader on a project may be called to task to explain the performance gap, or even be reprimanded for spearheading a failing effort. "We expected 5 percent improvement in the first thirty days." "You promised the new equipment would increase productivity by 10 percent." "We expected the reorganization to be completed in one hundred days," "The new equipment was supposed to be completely operational by now." The more vigilant an organization is about tracking performance, the more glaring such differences will become. Even if the change leader only tacitly or reluctantly accepted the charge from more senior leadership, but did not challenge the appropriateness of the time or performance metrics, he or she will be seen as being associated with, or accepting of, substandard performance or outright failure.

In addition to the personal consequences of seeming to do a poor change management job when one is actually doing reasonably well, or at least conforming to the expected learning trajectory, a danger exists that the change leader, or someone else, will be tempted to "tinker" with the project because of the apparent "slippage." If we falsely expected one set of outcomes but are observing another, less satisfactory set, the temptation might be to engage in "corrective" actions.

Thus leaders may revise training, interject some other program, change vendors, change leaders, shuffle staff, hire new consultants, or, as typically happens, increase the pressure on individuals to perform in the hope they will get to where the leaders thought they *should* be. In a worst-case scenario, leaders may even discard a change altogether, or replace it with a new one, having incorrectly concluded that "it's not working," when in fact, it was simply following a natural learning curve path. We are firmly convinced that a large number of jettisoned or abandoned changes would have worked out okay if only allowed to run their course. This only adds to the turmoil experienced by organizational members as new changes are introduced to "tweak" or replace changes that are thought to not be working.

DISTINGUISHING CAPACITY TO
CHANGE FROM MOTIVATION

We use the golf illustration to make our points with leaders, rather than going directly to an organizational example, for one very important reason. When we ask managers about the golfer's desire to adapt to the new golf club, they unanimously agree the desire is there, in other words, that motivation is *not* an issue. Golfers want to attain the lowest score possible! They do not "resist" the changes they believe are likely to improve their score; they embrace them.

Tiger Woods, clearly one of the all-time great golfers, whose abilities and motivation cannot be questioned, took more than a year to adjust to a change in his swing. As noted in the quotation at the beginning of this chapter, some people were beginning to write him off, others were looking for explanations in all the wrong places—he was adjusting to a self-imposed change, climbing the learning curve; his game afterward was better than ever.

Organizations often attribute the failure of change to individuals' lack of motivation, laziness, resistance, or worse. Our example raises the point that even when leaders don't need to worry about motivation, or can assume it to be high (for example, the highly committed employees discussed in the previous chapter), performance inevitably declines in the face of change. Ignoring this reality leads to a conspiracy of sorts in which people over-promise and under-deliver improvements associated with a planned change. The conspirators are the change leaders who demand the unrealistic and think they are getting it just because no one tells them otherwise; the leaders downstream who foolishly promise what they cannot deliver; and even vendors, consultants, or in-house staff groups who stand to gain by going along, or may suffer if they seem to oppose the change plan. When it comes to change initiatives from above, people are reluctant to say the emperor has no clothes, lest they be labeled "resistors."

If change leaders could only accept the fact that even the most motivated performers will follow "the laws of nature" when adapting to a change, then they could take motivation out of the equation as the sole or primary explanation for poor adaptation to change initiatives. This is a very important realization for managers.

"Resistance" to change implies volitional behavior, whereas "learning" implies involuntary physiological and psychological explanations for the behavior. "Resistance" implies negative attitudes, whereas "learning" implies positive movement. Certainly, motivation may still be an issue, as was discussed in Chapter 6, and resistance may still be real. Our point is, *at minimum,* performance following a change initiative (assuming the change involves a reasonably large change in people's work routines) is likely initially to reflect an adjustment factor, with motivational factors working in support of or opposition to this adjustment.

Leaders need to recognize these differential effects, plan for them, and implement steps to nurture the new behaviors in the direction of ramping up the new performance as rapidly as possible—addressing both learning and motivation aspects of people's performance. When you assume that motivation is the only performance issue (in other words, people always "resist" change) your responses are likely to be inappropriate (such as engaging in closer monitoring in lieu of offering more support or training). These inappropriate responses may create motivational problems where none previously existed.

COMBINING CAPACITY TO CHANGE
AND MOTIVATION TO CHANGE

Once a change is introduced, both the content (what is being done) as well as the process (how it's being done) quickly operate to shape people's beliefs about what is happening, leading to the exertion of effort on behalf of or against the change effort, as described in Chapter 6, on motivation. Such initial reactions may remain relatively stable over time (or at least throughout the change process), or they may shift as people gain more experience with the change. For example, people may decide this change is not as good or as bad as they had initially thought, or they may find they can perform at levels they previously thought they couldn't, or be surprised that this time management has provided adequate support and genuine rewards and recognitions.

These assessments operate either to create a motivational boost to do what is necessary to overcome the "capacity to learn" barriers to change, that is, putting effort into mastering the change as quickly as possible, thus accelerating the slope of the recovery curve, or to decelerate the recovery curve and prolong the duration of performance problems subsequent to a change. To the degree this motivation ebbs over time, so will behavioral support for the change or, to the degree that motivation improves over time, so will behavioral support.

In some cases, however, the motivational calculus may support "anti-change" behaviors (resistance, sabotage, stonewalling of events as they unfold), causing change-appropriate behaviors to suffer to the point that periods of low performance are prolonged. This can result in the failure to achieve change goals or ending up with performance that may even be worse than before the change. If, however, the costs of noncompliance are very high, individuals may display behaviors that appear to be compliant with the change requirements. The downside is they may do only the minimum required, harbor negative attitudes that will manifest themselves in other ways (passive resistance, subversive behaviors toward the change, refusal to help others), or adversely react to future change demands (recall our discussion of compliance versus influence from Chapter 4).

In Figure 7.3 we combine the learning effects just discussed with the motivational effects discussed in Chapter 6 to look at the ultimate performance consequences once a change is introduced. If the solid line represents the inevitable performance issues associated with learning new things, then the dotted lines above and below represent the motivational boost or decrement that will either shorten or lengthen the duration of the performance recovery. (Although we've depicted the performance changes as straight lines on all our graphs, in reality, these are probably best thought of as curves having multiple inflection points, representing positive or negative motivational forces as the situation unfolds.)

Again, as we noted in our discussion of motivation, the learning effects depicted by our performance curves can also be thought of at the generic, "average person" level, or at the level of specific individuals. Certainly people differ in their capacity to learn new tasks, in their motivation and various individual characteristics as we discussed earlier, and in their initial performance level, yielding different curves for different people.

As with our discussion of individual differences in the previous chapter, our goal is not to force leaders to entertain as many individual scenarios as they

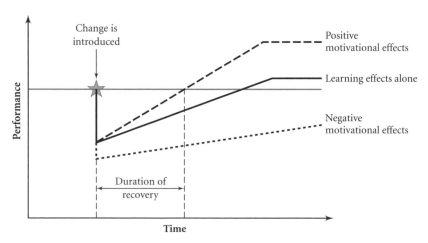

Figure 7.3. Combined learning and motivational effects on post-change performance

have people working with them. Rather, it is to show the benefits of raising the types of questions we've raised here and thus having a more realistic view of human behavior to guide our thinking about change. Further, there are times leaders need to resort to an individual-level analysis—when they anticipate that one or more people's performance during change may be problematic, or when they are concerned about the performance of one or more individuals key to the success of the change.

APPLYING THE FRAMEWORK

Let us illustrate how this framework may be used to focus our thinking about an upcoming change. Although our examples are at the "group" level, a similar case can be made for any one individual's performance during change.

Basic Parameters

If leaders consider the basic elements of the framework, in other words, depth of performance decline and duration of the recovery, and how motivation may affect the slope of the learning curve, what information can they bring to bear? Given the degree to which they have done this kind of change before (for example, a technology change, a reorganization, the implementation of a new customer service program), what do they know (or can find out) about the likely disruption? For instance, if the last call center consolidation created havoc for several weeks, why do they think the next one will be uneventful? If they have an answer as to why, so be it; if they don't have a good answer, maybe a more realistic performance curve would be in order. It amazes us how organizations can suffer total amnesia from one change to the other.

If the change is truly unique, can leaders still take a stab at its component parts and why they think these will or will not cause a performance dip? Can they find other organizations that have gone through the same change and capture their experience? What makes leaders think that their environment will produce similar or dissimilar results? How will they need to factor what they've learned into their planning?

Motivationally, what is the state of the organization? Are people enthused by the change; generally upbeat about the organization's direction; and possessing the skills, energy, and abilities to focus on the change at hand? Or are people tired, cynical, stretched too thin, and not quite up to the demands of the change? The answers to such questions may help predict two different performance paths a given change may take (as depicted in Figure 7.3). Subsequent to such an analysis, leaders may reexamine their plans, consider means of addressing motivational issues, or set their sights lower for how much change is possible, and how fast. In essence, this is what the framework used throughout the book has been leading up to: WHAT is to be changed, by WHOM, and in what CONTEXT, and how these will need to be reflected in change leaders' consideration of whether they need to modify their ideas and how to best proceed.

Manipulating Parameters

What if you want to affect one or more aspects of your change projection? In Figure 7.4 we show how two possible adjustments, prior training of existing staff (Figure 7.4a) or the addition of extra staff (Figure 7.4b), may be used to dampen the performance decline due to learning effects at the time of the change. Namely, the performance decline will not be as severe if people have already learned some of the routines off-line, or if they have more time to focus on the change because some of their day-to-day routines are handled by others. However, the recovery curves differ for the two interventions. In this illustration, early training yielded milder declines and quicker recovery. The choice of an intervention could then be based on the availability of resources as well as a cost-benefit analysis of the different alternatives. Of course, other interventions may give the same or similar results (for example, improved tools, ongoing coaching, quick troubleshooting of problems, and so on).

A good example of affecting the learning curve parameters through a troubleshooting intervention can be found in Toyota's approach to manufacturing changes. When such changes are introduced, technical SWAT teams are deployed throughout the plant. The purpose of these teams is to provide the necessary support for any area where change-related problems are occurring. In addition, they are responsible for determining what engineering or manufacturing modifications are necessary to permanently fix the problems that have arisen. Toyota fully anticipates that performance right after a change will de-

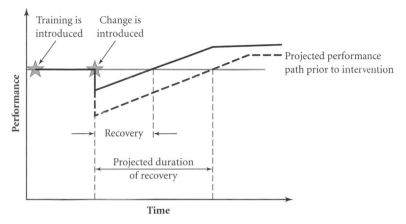

A. Implementation of Early Training

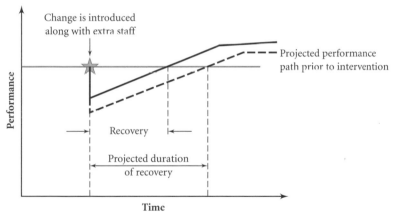

B. Provision of Extra Resources

Figure 7.4. Ameliorating adjustment problems through the implementation of early training versus the provision of extra resources

cline. However, it minimizes the depth and duration of that decline through the additional resources made available to help in the period right after the change. The additional resources are obviously not free, but Toyota has a reputation for ramping up production twice as fast as other car companies. They apparently see a favorable cost benefit!

Metrics

One by-product of this discussion of plotting how performance will progress during a change should be a better appreciation for the importance of tracking changes so that one knows what is going on. As the old saying goes, if you don't have a plan, any road will get you there. Well, if you don't have an expectation of how the change should proceed, or an unrealistic one, how will you know if you are doing okay or not?

Depending on the nature of the change, the metrics may be more or less precise. A technology change should be accompanied by a projection of how production or services should be affected, which can usually be assessed in terms of efficiency, transactions handled, speed, downtime, and so on. In contrast, a reorganization may be much more difficult to track. Yet leaders can still make an effort to project what the indicators should be as to whether things are going well or not. This is where surveys of employees, customers (internal or external), or vendors may be used to get the pulse of the change.

If you have realistic projections of the performance trajectory, as well as reasonable metrics for tracking, you will be better able to decide if appropriate progress is being made, whether additional tweaking is actually needed, or whether you should pull the plug before things go much further. This will protect you from knee-jerk reactions based on the perceived performance gap between the "myth" and the reality (shown in Figure 7.2), as well as help you decide if you should stay the course even though you are struggling with performance issues.

When managing projects of any kind, it is understood that having project milestones, metrics, and timelines is essential for intelligent and less emotional project-related decision making. Change implementation is a project management challenge. Having metrics, performance projections, timetables, and milestones should improve your decision making and your success rate.

CONCLUSION

In this chapter we have addressed an important determinant of performance subsequent to a change—humans' capacity to adapt. Leaders need to give up the notions that humans are able to "turn on a dime," quickly engage in new behaviors, and not miss a beat, while at the time managing to meet all of their organizational responsibilities, even as new demands are placed on them. Instead, leaders should ask the following questions:

- What is the best, most realistic estimate of the adaptation difficulties people are likely to face with the new requirements? What do we know or need to find out about people's skills and abilities, competing demands for their attention, resources available, and evidence from previous changes that would lead us to have confidence in our assessment?

- What are the consequences of letting the adaptation process take its course? If we think in terms of the depth of decline and duration of the performance recovery, we may have business reasons for wanting to better manage these (for example, certain declines in quality or customer service may not be acceptable and may need to be protected against).

- If these consequences are not acceptable, how can we better manage the adaptation process? For example, provide more training, especially before implementation; remove distractions; or provide more support?

- How will we track the degree to which adaptation is taking place as per plan, and what metrics will we use?

- How do we best communicate our assessment of how the adaptation process is likely to proceed so as to better prepare the organization for what will *realistically* take place or to negotiate for the appropriate resources to ensure performance to plan?

- How do we push back when others ignore the realities of human learning and make unreasonable demands, or provide unreasonable timetables for implementing change (besides retelling our golfing tale)?

8

CHANGE DOES NOT OCCUR

IN A VACUUM

"The importance of culture. It can't be underestimated."
Julie Roehm, fired Wal-Mart marketing executive[1]

In previous chapters, our discussions have been all about the change—what is to be changed, who will lead the change, and who is expected to adopt the change. In this chapter we consider the last important component of our change model, namely, the CONTEXT in which the change and its participants are embedded. Many leaders, when deciding on a change, fail to adequately consider surrounding factors that may influence the likelihood of successful implementation. Were they to undertake such a situational analysis, they might alter their assessment of the probability of success to the point of modifying or even totally rethinking their change plans.

This contextual analysis encompasses two levels—the business environment in which the organization operates and the various components that make up the organization's internal environment. Decisions about what to change and how to go about it are affected by both contexts. For example, when planning major changes that will probably create a great deal of uncertainty for highly skilled segments of the workforce (for example, the merger of two finance organizations or the outsourcing of technical work), leaders would be remiss if they didn't take labor market conditions into account. During expansionary times, employees testing the waters for new opportunities may find that they are very marketable and thus choose to leave rather than stay to help implement the change.

Similarly, when considering a change that requires major modifications in people's routines, leaders may conclude that its probability of success is lessened due to the many ongoing changes already in progress, changes that will distract people's attention from the target change or that will sour them on the prospects for positive change. For example, after a string of recalls embarrassed Toyota and threatened to tarnish its reputation for quality, it did something unusual. To give the quality program a better chance of succeeding, Toyota "tapped the brakes" on the introduction of new models. One model's U.S. introduction was delayed for a year "to ensure that American workers have the time to learn how to build the model without glitches."[2] Compare this with the "too much too fast" approach at Ford cited in Chapter 1.

These two examples point to the fact that "context" for any particular change encompasses elements both external and internal to the organization. The external context represents the environment in which the organization is embedded, various aspects of which may have an impact on change success, and thus should affect change planning. In our current treatment of the external context, there is no way of outlining which specific external factor may affect a particular planned change. Therefore, we simply want to highlight the importance of doing an external environmental analysis by touching on several factors that may facilitate or hinder a change. Subsequently, our main focus for this chapter will be to delve into the critical internal context issues that may significantly affect change efforts.

KEY EXTERNAL ENVIRONMENT CONSIDERATIONS

Although the notion of an organization's "external environment" could mean almost anything that's "out there," in the following text we highlight a few key environmental factors that can affect change plans. As we noted, while these factors should be considered for possible impact on one's change ideas, the specific aspect of each that may prove to be important is a function of the overall situation facing the organization and the nature of the specific change being considered.

For example, a company operating in a highly constrained vendor environment (in other words, is highly dependent on a single or few vendors) would need to carefully consider the vendor's capability and willingness to cooperate with planned changes in manufacturing, inventory, or logistics. Conversely, the same company making other changes may need to carefully consider local labor markets, regulations, or the broader economic environment. In the following, we illustrate the types of questions one can ask about each major external environmental factor.

Labor markets—Will the quantity, quality, mobility, or degree of unionization affect the change implementation? For example, airlines have been able to institute draconian changes because industry dynamics provide few alternatives to those who choose to remain in the industry. In contrast, the competition for people in the biological sciences could create an exodus of talent if firms in that industry even attempted to implement similar changes.

Legal and regulatory factors—Will the proposed change run into legal or regulatory challenges, or are the legal or regulatory environments in transition such that they may turn out to affect the planned change? For example, many a reorganization has been challenged on the basis of age, sex, or race discrimination. Leaders should anticipate such reactions and include them in their change strategizing.

Economic factors—How may broad economic conditions affect one's ability to implement the change or people's reactions to it? If, for example, economic conditions are starting to force you into cost-cutting programs, how will these affect the resources available for change support and people's attitudes toward the change? For instance, high gasoline prices are motivating employees to now seriously consider working at least some days from home (telecommuting). What are the implications, if any, of more people in the targeted unit not being on site every day?

Affiliated organizations—Which organizations are important for making the change work, and what do we know about how they will respond? Labor union leaders tend to become more militant (that is, opposed to management changes) as union elections draw nearer. If the change depends on a vendor's capability, shouldn't you investigate the vendor's track record and ability to deliver? How many times have you heard the software "wasn't ready on time" or "had bugs in it"? Although there are many potential explanations for such events, if they happen repeatedly, should they not be part of your change strategizing?

Technology environment—To what extent does the change effort depend on events associated with the technology involved, and how can you factor those into your thinking? For example, the reliability and complexity of the technology may have major consequences for change plans. As we've already noted, every Enterprise Resource Planning (ERP) change that we are familiar with has taken twice as long and cost twice as much as anticipated. These data are widely available. Yet rarely is this evidence incorporated into change planning.

Demographics—How will your change be affected by generational, cultural, geographic, educational, or other trends? Relocating a plant in order to reduce labor costs or escape labor unions may turn out not to be the solution hoped for as one finds that the skill levels, education levels, or work experiences of employees in the new location bring new problems that may outweigh the benefits of the lower labor costs. For instance, it took Mercedes Benz several years to rectify quality problems at its new, rural Alabama plant.

Regional and national cultures—What about the local culture may affect the implementation of the change or the transportability of a change that worked elsewhere? Although there has been a great deal of interest recently in how cultures, especially national cultures, differ, much less is known about how such differences affect reactions to change attempts. Different cultures have different orientations toward managerial authority, leadership styles, and new technology, as well as individuals' expectations about work-related conditions and outcomes. Such differences need to be incorporated into change strategizing.

For example, as Toyota expands globally, it is finding that local cultures react differently to programs and changes that have worked well in Japan, making the spread of the Toyota Way somewhat spotty. Still, Toyota's leaders feel they must prevent "the Toyota Way from getting more and more diluted as Toyota grows overseas."[3] But as they push these changes globally, they find that local cultures may have difficulty accepting practices such as morning calisthenics or allowing line workers to halt the assembly line when they spot a defect. Such cultural forces slow down the spread of the corporate culture into new national cultures, creating problems with training, quality, and implementation of new programs.

Although with increased globalization the emphasis has been on differences in national cultures, differences in local or regional cultures should not be ignored. For example, as Hewlett-Packard (HP) grew and began to enjoy great success and admiration in Silicon Valley, the time came to expand to other parts of the country. The company quickly found that its aura did not travel well. In Loveland, Colorado, a ranching town, the transferred HP workers began "stealing girlfriends and wives, driving up real estate prices, and increasingly dominating local politics," thus alienating locals. The founders then decided that in the future, offices would be placed in areas of affluent and well-educated populations in order to minimize culture clashes.[4]

In summary, organizations are embedded in economic, legal, social, cultural, and demographic environments, and elements of these may impinge on organizational efforts to implement change. Change leaders would be well-advised to do an environmental scan and then use the results to make decisions about whether or how to proceed, either by modifying or rethinking the contemplated change, or making collateral changes first before proceeding with the contemplated change.

THE INTERNAL CONTEXT

One of the difficulties in dealing with the concept of an internal organizational context or environment is to reduce it to meaningful subdimensions. By definition, "context" could refer to almost anything. Thus the organizational context consists of everything from the color of the walls to the nature of various systems (such as measurement and reward) to the quality and quantity of resources and the shared beliefs and values that form the organization's culture.

Given the many ways of describing an organization's internal context, we will focus on three specific aspects that are critical in shaping change events: the human and physical resources available to effect the change; the organization's culture; and the turbulence or disruption created by other, ongoing changes. Might other aspects of an organization's internal context have some influence on change events? Probably so; but these are, as far as we have seen, the "biggies."

Resources

The first contextual consideration we want to touch on is the question of resources. Time and time again we've seen organizations initiate changes requiring certain expertise only to realize that the most recent layoff or outsourcing decision meant that these resources were no longer available. Similarly, it's tough to train people in preparation for a change when the organization is already understaffed and the remaining people are still responsible for the same, or greater, workloads.

It's going to be difficult to install new software throughout the organization, or any other new system, when people are already stretched so thin that they are unlikely to be able to devote the attention the new systems require. Although it may seem obvious, change leaders need to consider the economic, physical, and human resources needed to make their change plan work and ask whether those are likely to be available. If not, they may have to cycle back through the feedback loops in our change model and either reconsider or modify the change plan.

Years ago, when General Motors bought EDS, a technology firm (which it has since sold), it hoped to have a captive source for spearheading improvements in plant technology. One project tackled by the EDS consultants was the replacement of the paper build-out sheets, or manifests, that were stuck under a car's windshield wiper as it moved down the assembly line. These sheets specified special equipment, type of interior, colors, and other features to be built into the car. The checking of these manifests, in order to ensure the right parts, represented a major problem. Some were damaged from the frequent handling, some fell off and disappeared altogether, some wound up missing pages, and assembly line workers sometimes had trouble remembering the specifications on the manifest as they went to retrieve and install the proper part.

The EDS solution was a small monitor located at each workstation that would constantly display the specifications for the car presently in front of the line worker. This put all the information right in front of him and kept it there for the duration of the time he worked on the car. He could refer to it as many times as he wanted, and it was not subject to damage as the car proceeded down the assembly line. The prototyping was done and the results looked encouraging, though the cost was substantial. At the one plant we visited, the time had come to train people on the new system. However, the plant manager's response was that with the production targets he had been given, and the staff cuts he had endured, there was no way he was going to free up people from the line to attend the training. Needless to say, without the appropriate training, the system failed to perform as expected.

Organizational Culture

The concept of corporate culture is firmly entrenched in our management lexicon, made popular by business books such as *In Search of Excellence, Built to Last,* and *Good to Great.* When we couple the words *culture* and *change,* however, we find an interesting anomaly. Many people talk about "changing culture," but far fewer people consider culture's effect *on* change. Yet cultural issues are often given as explanations for difficulties with changes such as mergers or acquisitions, the inability to transport practices across companies or even divisions of the same company, or the performance of leaders across settings.

One aspect of culture that we and others have found to be more and more important as organizations undertake ever-more-frequent changes is the prevailing level of cynicism. When cynicism about the organizations' motives, track record, or the future success of a given change effort is deeply rooted, individuals will be less inclined to exert energy in support of the change. This is why so many of us have heard the refrains "change du jour," "it too shall pass," or "flavor of the month" when organizational members react to change. These are reflections of a culture that has become cynical about change initiatives. In our own work, we have repeatedly found that a culture of cynicism translates directly into less commitment to proposed changes. This seems to happen regardless of the type of change being considered.

Although *culture* represents a largely intangible characteristic of organizations, it is generally viewed as the pattern (more or less pervasive) of the basic assumptions, values, and beliefs adopted by organizational members over time because they were found to be effective in addressing the problems or environments faced by the organization. Thus we talk of types of culture (such as egalitarian, entrepreneurial, bureaucratic, ethical, innovative, and so on). As such, a change involving greater centralization of power and resources will engender a much stronger, negative reaction in a free-wheeling, entrepreneurial, and individualistic culture than in a highly structured, bureaucratic one. Conversely, a change involving new directions, new opportunities, and challenges to the status quo would be received more positively within an entrepreneurial culture.

For example, what brought Julie Roehm to the attention of Wal-Mart was her reputation, during five years at Chrysler, for pushing the envelope in her marketing campaigns. At the time, Wal-Mart wanted to change its image and recruited her to be senior vice president of marketing. The "edgy" Ms. Roehm landed in Bentonville, Arkansas, took one look at Wal-Mart's drab, gray, windowless offices, consistent with the "everyday low prices" culture; grabbed a ladder and some paint; and proceeded to paint her office chartreuse with chocolate-brown trim. It was downhill from there.

As she and her counterparts in marketing pushed for trendier clothes to be carried in the stores, the merchandisers resisted, and asked for more signage advertising low prices. The old-timers were digging in and thwarting the efforts of this outsider. Eleven months after her arrival, she was gone. Asked what she learned from the experience, she replied, "The importance of culture. It can't be underestimated."[5]

Charles Schwab, the discount broker, bought U.S. Trust, a venerable, 150-year-old investment firm that catered to the rich, in the hopes of better reaching and serving that market. However, problems soon developed as the old-world, white-glove culture of U.S. Trust clashed with the populist culture of the discount brokerage world. There were disagreements over bonus payments, customer service, and even whether or not to dress in costumes for corporate events. Defections among U.S. Trust executives and a deterioration in its business soon followed. An industry consultant likened the merger to "Wal-Mart buying Neiman Marcus."[6] Several years later, Schwab divested itself of U.S. Trust.

Bob Nardelli came to Home Depot and from the beginning showed disdain for the culture built by the founders—one based on customer service, respect for individuals, promotion from within, and collegiality. He symbolically failed to meet or seek the inputs of the founders, though they were revered by the employees and lived in the same city; he forced out many executives who had come up through the ranks—a culturally valued career path; he imposed tight controls on store managers who were weaned on heavy doses of autonomy and local control. He hired ex-military officers to bring order to what he saw as a loose culture; he replaced full-time store employees with part-timers, hurting customer service, a deeply held cultural value. He too is gone, the announcement of his departure reportedly greeted with applause in the stores!

Detect a pattern yet? Think of culture as the organization's immune system. It is meant to protect it from intrusions and to regulate day-to-day functioning. When change is introduced, *if it is seen as an attack on basic and valued aspects of the organism,* the immune system will go into rejection mode. It may not always win, but you'd be foolish to bet against it. At best, you will be dealing with a long-lasting and debilitating infection. Sometimes, when aspects of culture imperil the organization's survival (domestic automobile companies, legacy airlines), the organization needs heavy doses of immunity-suppressing drugs (for example, bankruptcy). Fortunately, not all changes are seen as "attacks" on the culture. Thus cultural aspects may be the source of rejection, they may be supportive of the change because it is consistent with the prevailing values, or they may be benign if the change does not engage them.

Change Turbulence

Although people have long recognized the difficulties created by turbulent organizational environments, this understanding has been largely limited to the effects of external forces, and their volatility, on the functioning of entire organizations. If we apply this concept to individual organizations, we can think of change turbulence as the internal volatility being experienced by organizational members, in other words, the frequency and severity of other changes going on, that may buffet them as they try to implement a particular change.

We may think of this in terms of a river kayaking analogy. It is one thing to paddle in a relatively calm river, with only occasional outcroppings that have to be navigated. It is quite another to paddle the same kayak in a raging river with large boulders jutting out everywhere. In a sense, some organizational changes take place in the white waters of a raging river made up of too many changes being pushed too fast and too close together.

This has important implications for change leaders. Even if they carefully think through what they want to change, with whom, and how, if they leave out the level of change turbulence they may be disappointed by a surprising, negative reaction to their careful planning. In such cases, leaders find that people's reactions to the focal change (for example, resistance) are really better understood in terms of the surrounding changes; they are colored by the fact that people see themselves as careening from change to change.

If we think of a current change as embedded in a variety of other, ongoing changes, we can utilize the learning curve and motivation models from Chapters 6 and 7 to illustrate the impact of change turbulence on people's motivation and capacity to change. In Figure 8.1, we illustrate the impact of interrupting the performance recovery from "Change 1" by introducing another change, "Change 2," and then another change, "Change 3." Each change requires the expenditure of physical, emotional, and cognitive resources, and as these resources get diverted to new changes they are unavailable for application to the previous changes, prolonging the duration of the recovery to baseline and the realization of performance improvements. Furthermore, each change following on the heels of a previous yet only partially digested or mastered change starts from a lower performance baseline.

In terms of motivation, we can see how the stress and frustration of not being able to focus on a given change before being distracted by other changes, and being perpetually in a "catch-up" mode, will decrease people's motivation to work hard on behalf of subsequent changes. In essence, many people in today's organizations spend much of their time "under water," gasping to catch their breath from one change to another. The observations that "people naturally resist change" or "people are tired of change" or "people around here are catatonic" (or "shell-shocked" or "playing possum," and so on) reflect the toll

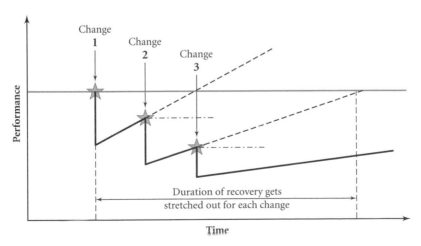

Figure 8.1. The cumulative effect of overlapping changes on performance recovery

extracted by multiple and overlapping changes to which people have been forced to adjust.

People have a finite capacity to adapt to change. It's up to change leaders how they choose to best utilize this capacity. They can try to focus it on important changes, and thus achieve performance recovery and improvement as efficiently as possible. Or they can dissipate this capacity in a barrage of changes, thereby detracting from any one change and damaging overall organizational performance.

We have found that most people resonate with this scenario of frequent and overlapping changes sapping energy from the really important changes, feeling that it accurately describes their day-to-day working lives. What, then, can be done? One thing that can be done is to go into a "planned change" mode in which changes are not viewed independently, but rather are put in the context of other changes already in progress or contemplated.

Imagine a "war room" where the various changes, their impact, required resources, implementation hurdles, and progress are plotted. In this "war room," all existing and contemplated changes have a timeline, a launch date, expected performance decline and recovery data, and other change details posted on the walls. Key managers are brought together to assess progress, identify potential and actual problems, and negotiate mid-course corrections. Stepping back and looking at all the changes tackled by the organization at the same time allows us to detect, address, and prevent change overload and its accompanying dysfunctional consequences.

So many "projects" in organizations (construction projects, software projects, location changes, engineering projects, and so on) receive the full treatment of project planning, budgeting, development of time and progress milestones, assignment of project managers (often specifically trained in project management techniques), and even the application of sophisticated project planning and tracking tools. Yet it always amazes us that many major organizational changes, such as reorganizations or acquisitions, do not receive the benefits of similar attention, with leadership often seemingly "flying by the seat of their pants."

Examining a *portfolio of changes,* leaders can then prioritize changes in terms of their centrality to business strategy, financial impact, likelihood of success, or whatever other criteria are chosen. On the basis of such prioritization, leaders can space changes better; they can rearrange their sequence; they can eliminate less essential ones; they can improve change support or leadership so that earlier changes take hold more quickly, allowing for subsequent changes to be considered. If they do some of these things, the graph in Figure 8.1 might now look more like Figure 8.2.

Essentially, change leaders are trying to balance two countervailing forces: on the one hand, the need to drive change through their organizations if they are to respond to ever-changing environments, and on the other the importance of incorporating what they know about the human aspects of change. If they let the former blind them to the latter, they are doomed to failed change efforts, as has tended to be the case for many organizations. It is all too easy to say that all changes are "essential." They may be so in theory, but what if in practice most fail to realize their objectives and some crash and burn, while the organization suffers from change overload?

The notion of planned change, subjecting change ideas to rigorous screening, putting resources behind those that survive the screen, and carefully nurturing change progress in concert with the organization's change capacity could (should) become a cultural value. Companies we admire for being able

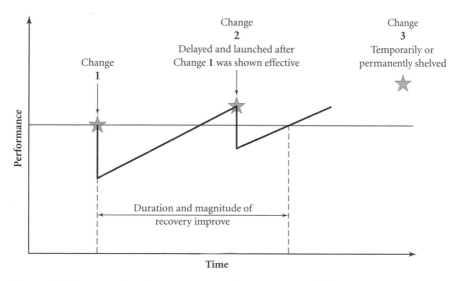

Figure 8.2. Rearranging changes so as to reduce change turbulence

to reinvent themselves and stay near the top for long periods of time, such as GE, have shown themselves to have change-focused and change-capable cultures. Their change capabilities are built into a system for managing change that is integrated with the various operating systems of the company, in which each change is viewed as one of a portfolio of changes to be managed using project management techniques that are used for other projects.

In our own research, we have found that one of the most consistent findings is the negative impact of change turbulence on change reactions—*change turbulence saps support from the change at hand regardless of how well-planned or executed the change may be.*[7] Incorporating the notion of change turbulence into change thinking requires that leaders understand the following:

- Organizational changes cannot be contemplated as independent, isolated events. The restructuring is not independent of the new technology implementation, which is not independent of the ongoing consolidation of functions brought on by the merger, which is not independent of the manufacturing changes necessitated by the launching of the new product. Individuals react to the totality of their change environment.

- All changes cannot be "priority 1." Leaders need to take a more strategic view of the total portfolio of changes being considered. Which is most central to achieving the business strategy? Which is likely to yield the greatest benefits? Which is likely to pave the way for other, future changes?

- No matter how carefully leaders contemplate a given change, the actual benefits (if any) will be a function of the change environment in which it is embedded. Turbulent environments may negate many, if not all, of the hoped-for benefits.

- The challenges associated with implementing a given change will increase exponentially as the environment in which the change is to be embedded becomes more turbulent.

- Not all individuals will react the same way to change turbulence (as noted in Chapter 6, in our discussion of emotional stability). To the degree that they can, leaders may want to be more selective about whom they put in environments characterized by frequent and overlapping changes.

- Senior leadership needs to take seriously its role of orchestrating the various change initiatives. Although each functional area may want to launch its own changes, only senior leadership, working together, can keep too many boulders from falling into the river and upsetting the kayaks. We speak of the value of portfolio management when it comes to investments and innovation projects. Leaders need to apply portfolio management thinking to their many changes.

CONCLUSION

In this chapter we've asked the reader to do something few books or articles about change discuss: namely, consider not just the change but also the context in which it will be embedded. No matter how well-thought-out the change idea may be, even if it's perfectly consonant with an analysis of the business strategy, leadership capabilities, follower characteristics, and resources at hand, it will not be implemented in a vacuum. Instead, various characteristics of the organization's internal and external environment will act to either enhance or detract from the change effort.

A consideration of external and internal environments should again reinforce a point we've made several times already about why being a "copycat" doesn't work when it comes to change. If two organizations do not operate in the same external environments, or have similar internal environments, why would one expect the same results for a given change? Environments can be seen as benign, facilitative, or hostile for changes.

We reminded the reader that external to the organization, labor markets, economic conditions, legal and regulatory affairs, technology, demographics, and regional or national cultures can all affect the success of a change effort. Internal to the organization, we focused on three major contextual factors to be considered: the organization's resources, its culture, and the level of change turbulence being experienced.

In summary, change leaders need to look beyond the particulars of the change they are working on. They need to consider the factors inside and outside the organization that may enhance or impede efforts on behalf of the change. Savvy leaders try to anticipate these influences in arriving at their decision to proceed, reconsider, or change something else first.

9

PUTTING THE PIECES TOGETHER

"The proper metaphor for managing change is balancing a mobile. . . . The key to the change effort is not attending to each piece in isolation; it's connecting and balancing all the pieces."

D. J. Duck[1]

Many change leaders, comfortable with their assessment of a business situation, proceed by trying to convince others, gently or not so gently, that they have an appropriate response for fixing the problem they perceive to exist. What they're saying is, "Here is my vision" (well-articulated or not), "now let's implement it." Throughout this book we have promoted a more deliberative process, stressing the multiple considerations that go into the diagnosis and analysis of a change situation before one can make a determination about the advisability or nature of change initiatives. Thus we've raised the issues of WHAT needs to be changed and why, WHO is likely to lead and WHO is likely to be asked to follow, and what is the CONTEXT, both internal and external.

Having advocated this more complex approach to analyzing change situations, let us now address how change leaders can apply it in arriving at a decision of whether to go forth with the contemplated change, modify the proposed change, or first work to alter the situation in preparation for the targeted change. We will do so through the posing of key questions to ask at the various junctures of our model (replicated in Figure 9.1)—the answers to such questions *pointing* toward a course of action.

The reason we say "pointing" toward a course of action is that by now the reader should be well aware of how complex change situations really are, and of the many combinations and permutations of factors that can facilitate or hinder a change effort.

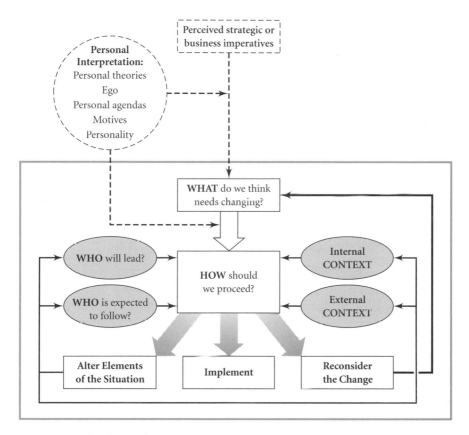

Figure 9.1. The change framework

The process of moving from a perceived business problem to a well-implemented change response is not simple or linear. Rather, it can be a very challenging, convoluted, two-steps-forward-one-step-back path with plenty of surprises and miscalculations. The difference between successful and not-so-successful change leaders is the degree to which they acknowledge the complexity of the task up front, and make an effort to comprehend the problem, analyze the situation, and custom-tailor the response.

Sometimes leaders reach a snap decision about what to change and impatiently want others to embrace their idea, though they have not taken the effort to fully understand the situation. In such situations, they are trying to take a shortcut from the realization of a business problem to the implementation of a solution, traveling the "down-the-middle" path of the model (sticking to the white boxes, not venturing into the gray ovals)—"Here is what's going on"; "I know what needs to change"; "Now you change"; often followed by, "Why don't they understand the need to make this change?"

By jumping quickly from the problem to the fix, change leaders may suffer from several blind spots. First, they may be unaware of the extent to which either their assessment of the problem or its intended solution may have major flaws. Second, if their assessment of the problem is correct, they may not have fully explored other alternatives that might address it. Third, if they've done a good job of assessing the problem and finding a corresponding solution, in the abstract, they may not be sufficiently aware of the WHO and CONTEXT factors that might seriously affect change implementation.

Thus Bob Nardelli was correct in his assessment that Home Depot needed improved controls such as better information systems; Carly Fiorina was correct in her assessment that HP needed stronger service and PC businesses; Jacques Nasser understood that Ford needed to become more globally diversified. Similarly, almost every fired or beleaguered change leader was probably pursuing one or more initiatives that made excellent sense given the nature of the business problem faced.

Such leaders rarely lose their jobs or influence because their ideas had little merit; rather, they lose their jobs because they don't fully consider the following: WHO am I and what do I bring to the table? WHO are the people I'm depending on to make this happen? What about the internal CONTEXT makes me think this will or will not go smoothly? What is going on in the external CONTEXT that I need to take into account? How do I use these factors to help build a workable match between what I believe needs to be done and what the organization can realistically achieve?

In other words, as we've said earlier, good strategy with poor change strategizing may get you nowhere, or even fired. Good business strategy that has been vetted through change strategizing is far more likely to lead to success. Let us proceed with an examination of the types of questions to be asked at each stage of our model that will point toward the decision of whether to change, what to change, and how to proceed.

WHAT DO YOU THINK NEEDS CHANGING?

This stage of one's thinking about initiating change is perhaps the most critical. Everything flows from it, yet leaders often see a one-to-one correspondence between a business problem and a solution that may or may not be there. As we remind many managers, "Thou shall reorganize" is not the eleventh commandment. Nor is every merger created in heaven, or every IT or quality program implementation the end-all for what ails you, nor are layoffs the only solution to a profit squeeze.

As we noted in Chapter 2, moving from business imperative to WHAT needs changing is often an educated guess that needs to be reality and evidence tested. The five critical questions leaders need to ask at this point are

1. What is the nature of the business problem we are trying to address via the change, and how confident are we of this assessment?

2. Why do we think this change will address that problem, and what other alternatives might accomplish the same goal?

3. Have we considered the ramifications of this choice, performed even a rough cost-benefit analysis, and benchmarked it against our, or other organizations', experiences when making similar changes?

4. Have we looked at our own personal biases, preconceptions, uncertainties, personal agendas, or ego issues that may have shaped our interpretation of events and assessment of remedies?

5. Have we reality tested our assessment and our remedy with other, knowledgeable and trusted colleagues (not just those who agree with our view of the situation, or are subject to our positional power)? Are there good "devil's advocates" available?

Basically, this phase implores the change leader to be not only strategic but also introspective, even soul-searching, inclusive of others, and creative in the generation and consideration of alternatives. Whereas we often hear how important it is to involve others for the sake of smoothing the implementation of change, it is equally important to include others in order to protect the quality of the chosen change initiative. In fact, in certain situations, the exact nature of the change may not be as important as the fact that a change was derived through a process wherein those charged with implementation saw the proposed change as valid.

For example, if there is a need to shake up a sleepy organization that has lost its way or is about to, the exact nature of the change may not be as important as the process used to arrive at a change. Thus the leader may have a perfectly good idea, but others' ideas generated at the leader's behest may be the better way to go, even if those ideas are not quite what the leader views as "optimal."

We all wear glasses of a particular color; we all bring personal biases to situations; we're all prisoners of our own backgrounds, personalities, training, and experiences; we all filter and interpret information in unique ways; we all have favorite decision-making and problem-solving approaches. At this point, the change leader is trying to validate the choice of a change before moving on and mapping it onto the various situational contingencies we've discussed.

Let us illustrate. When James McNerney was brought in as the new CEO of 3M, he quickly decided that Six Sigma, the vaunted GE quality program, was one aspect of WHAT the organization needed in order to introduce discipline into its various systems. Unfortunately, several years later, there are serious questions about whether or not the highly structured quality system, applied to every phase of the business, caused 3M to lose some of the innovative spirit for which it was famous and which has been largely credited with its success.

3M's current CEO, George Buckley, who has dismantled some of McNerney's initiatives, is quoted as saying, "Invention is by its very nature a disorderly process. . . . You can't put a Six Sigma process into that area and say, well, I'm getting behind on invention, so I'm going to schedule myself for three good ideas on Wednesday and two on Friday. That's not how creativity works."[2]

The point of this illustration is not to debate whether or not greater business discipline is good or bad, or whether quality programs are inherently threatening to innovation. Rather, as the new CEO, had McNerney asked himself about the nature of the problem he was trying to address, where and how that problem manifested itself in the organization, how his own long-term tenure at GE may have biased his perceptions of problems and solutions, and what some of the unintended consequences of his solutions might be, and had he reality-tested his ideas with those familiar with the long-term innovation tradition at the company, he might have reached different decisions as to the details of what he wanted to change, where, and at what cost.

The suitability of a change is a function of many factors. When outsiders walk in with a heightened sense of "certainty" because something worked for them before, they ought to tread carefully. New settings create uncertainty, and ideas need to be tested in ways they may not have had to be in other settings.

WHO SHALL LEAD THE CHANGE?

Having targeted a particular change option, the leader now asks who is in the best position to lead this particular change. This could be a matter of skills, both technical and change leadership skills; availability; trust; previous experience with similar changes; or particular attributes that are a "natural" for the change and the setting (for example, being credible in the particular situation). Some of the questions that can be asked about the leadership position are

1. Should the person who initiated the change also lead the change? Why or why not?

2. Will the person thought to be best to lead the change be able to see it through to the end, and could this change be made a portion of his or her responsibilities, with the provision of adequate support, rather than just a "sideline" that is heaped on an already full plate?

3. Will multiple organizational entities be affected by the change, and, therefore, should there be multiple change leaders?

4. What will be the key leadership challenges for this change effort (technical, structural, social, emotional, cultural, and so on)?

5. Which leaders possess the type of influence most likely to deal effectively with the identified leadership challenges (that is, why would people follow them more so than others)?

In other words, at this point leaders need to be introspective about their own capabilities, realistic about their influence "buckets," and honest about their other responsibilities, the likelihood of sticking it out with the change, and devoting the necessary time and effort. Too many good changes have died on the vine because the change leader simply proclaimed their arrival and didn't realize, till it was far too late, that little had changed ("I sent an e-mail about this three months ago. How come nothing has been done about it?").

Furthermore, at this juncture, the leader needs to be careful about specifying the skillsets of successful change leaders. The tendency is to select for the right technical skillset but not necessarily for the right social or change-savvy skills. One can always support gaps in the change leader's technical skills by putting people with these skills on the implementation team. One can rarely, however, make up for the lack of change savvy or credibility on the part of the person asked to lead the change; not only does that person need to be credible, he or she also needs to be open to feedback throughout the process and able and willing to make mid-course corrections.

Many examples can be found to illustrate how this part of the analysis could have been done differently by change leaders. Our earlier discussion of leadership influence and sources of credibility pointed to the problems when brand new leaders, lacking credibility in either the company or the industry, do not ally themselves with those who have internal credibility and involve them in change thinking.

But not all outsiders stumble. We have many examples, such as Gerstner at IBM and Hurd at HP, to illustrate that outsiders with change savvy or other sources of credibility can pull it off. Gordon Bethune, who transformed Continental Airlines, was able to gain support for his initiatives largely because his leadership style and influence "buckets" were "right on" for the setting (whereas they could have been less appropriate for driving major changes in another setting). Although he was new to Continental, he had "street credibility." He had been a mechanic in the Navy and had started in the airline business in maintenance. He was also a licensed commercial jet pilot, which helped him bridge the management-pilots gap so often found at airlines. Thus, though an "outsider," he connected well with major segments of his workforce and was able to gain acceptance for many of his initiatives.

We also have examples, such as Jager at P&G, Nasser at Ford, and Thoman at Xerox, in which insiders may not have been the right people to lead the change because they lacked change savvy. As a result, they were not able to influence others to follow them, or made it impossible for others to follow them because of the relentless and unrealistic pace of change, the lack of support, or the inability to foresee major barriers that would have to first be removed.

WHO IS EXPECTED TO ADOPT THE CHANGE?

This assessment asks the change leader to consider the characteristics of those expected to embrace the change. What is known about them that would suggest the change idea will be well-received or not? The following questions can help:

1. What evidence is there that people even see there is a problem?
2. How invested are the change targets in the current way of doing things?
3. What would be their motivation to stay the course versus adopt the change?
4. What are their perceptions of, attitudes toward, and commitments to the organization's and the leader's success?
5. Do they possess the necessary skills to master the desired new behaviors?
6. What would they require in terms of support in order to succeed?

This is the point at which leaders perform an assessment of the things they know or need to find out about the followers that would suggest barriers or enablers to the change effort. For example, are people likely to be concerned that they may not be able to master the new change, or even feel threatened by it? Are people's commitments to their profession, co-workers, or other entities likely to cause resistance to changes that might weaken such ties? Have people been doing things in a particular way for long periods of time with little evidence that there is a problem? Have people made such large investments (time, personal sacrifices, training, and so on) in the current way of doing things that they are likely to want to hold on to them? Will the change cause deterioration in their economic, psychological, physical, or social well being?

The point of these questions is *not* that one should only proceed with changes that people like. Rather, such assessments will often indicate the need for a reexamination of options concerning WHAT to change or begin to shape our thinking about HOW to proceed in ways that mitigate these factors.

An excellent example of a leader who apparently failed to correctly diagnose this aspect of the change setting is the director of the CDC, Dr. Julie Gerberding. In our earlier discussion of her change leadership, we noted that she tried to reorganize the CDC from what were basically pools of like-minded researchers and scientists focused on a problem (for example, specific infectious diseases) into cross-discipline and cross-interest groupings of people she thought would be better able to respond to particular public health threats.

However, even a casual analysis of the change targets should have made it clear that one of the major attractions of the CDC for scientists and researchers is the opportunity to work with colleagues who speak the same language and work on similar problems. To impose new structures that were more "top down" and which would disperse some of these groups across the organization should have been predicted to cause major morale problems. Had such an analysis been done, perhaps alternative, less disruptive solutions could have been found (such as cross-functional response teams that come together as needed), and more careful attention could have been paid to gaining the support of the affected scientists and researchers.

WHAT IS THE INTERNAL CONTEXT LIKE?

The leader is now ready to take the preceding observations about the WHAT and WHO and ask whether the change idea is likely to thrive or be stymied in the current organizational environment. Is the culture ready for the change? What are the competing pressures for people's attention? Does the infrastructure exist to support the change effort? The key questions to be asked at this juncture are

1. What is the fit between current organizational structures, systems, and processes and the proposed change?

2. What are the cultural factors that may oppose or support the proposed change?

3. What are the state and availability of the internal resources needed to support the change?

4. What is the organization's track record with implementing similar changes, or change in general?

5. What is the expected level of change turbulence? Is there too much currently on people's plates, and what other changes are being planned for the same time frame?

6. What are the levels of stress and cynicism within the targeted units?

Many change ideas are theoretically "good," but they just don't happen to fit with the current context. Given that, some of the leaders who we noted have failed to gain support for their change initiatives might not have any trouble with the very same initiatives in a different context. For instance, you cannot expect to do in a bureaucratic culture what you were able to do in a more flexible, professional culture; nor can you expect a traditional organization to embrace your calls for "out-of-the-box thinking." You also cannot expect people already overburdened by multiple changes to show a great deal of appetite for your latest initiative, no matter how sound it may be.

About the time we were finishing the manuscript for this book, Bob Nardelli, whose tenure at Home Depot has been used in several of our examples of change that was not handled well, was named CEO of Chrysler Corporation. This immediately raised the questions of why, and will it work? Using our model for diagnosing change situations, we are more optimistic about his chances for success at his new post.

Briefly, his experience in manufacturing at GE, especially in turning around lagging operations, will provide more credibility at another manufacturing company than it did at a retailer. As far as followers and context are concerned, the dire situation in the American automobile industry in general and at Chrysler in particular has created a readiness for major changes. This was not the case in the Home Depot environment, especially among the rank-and-file. In his new setting, the nature of the changes Nardelli has been identified with (and had a good track record with at GE)—Six Sigma, cost cutting, and manufacturing efficiencies—are probably what the doctor ordered, as most analysts agree that Chrysler needs to improve quality and efficiency.

Finally, a company whose private equity fund owners may have well-defined and perhaps narrow financial goals (for example, sell off pieces to recover some of their investment, or take the company public again), and one in which many of the executives and advisors have GE roots, should be easier for Nardelli to navigate than the more visible, public company environment that proved troublesome for him.

The question marks, and they are not trivial, are raised by two main issues. Though Nardelli wasn't a retailer, he drove off many of those with retail experience at Home Depot. In fact, 100 percent of his top 170 managers left during his tenure. He's not a "car guy," and repeating this type of purge at Chrysler could be disastrous, no matter how many ex-GE people he recruits. Second, his leadership style, variously described as "in your face," "friendly to facts and not people," or "imperial" could be a problem when it comes to dealing with the unions and in keeping and motivating enough of the "car guys" to stick around. Obviously, we have no way of predicting the future. However, this situation provides us with one more illustration of how setting-specific change issues really are. Thus leaders can succeed by carefully diagnosing situations and adjusting their approach accordingly, or they can seek a situation that better matches their approach. Nardelli may have done just that.

WHAT IS THE EXTERNAL CONTEXT LIKE?

Finally, the change leader takes all this information and assesses whether there are any factors in the organization's external environment that may help or hinder the change effort. Some of these may be clearly known, for example, the resistance of a union to certain restructuring attempts; others may be known with less certainty, such as changes in the availability or cost of certain essential resources; others may be totally unknown, yet contingency plans still need to be made for their occurrence, for example, will the next political elections create a more or less friendly environment for the proposed change? As we can see, the questions driving this assessment, by their nature, are less open to clear-cut answers, but we should contemplate them nonetheless.

1. What is the current state of the economic, business, political, regulatory, and social environments, and what do they mean for the change?

2. What is the state of the labor market, and how may this affect both the ability to attract the right people needed to support the change or the likelihood of losing employees who may seek work elsewhere?

3. What is the nature of the competitive business environment, and how might it affect change planning, execution, or flexibility?

4. What is the state of other organizations that may be essential for the change effort (such as vendors, consultants, and partners)?

These checks of the change planning take leaders beyond the confines of their organization, an arena in which they can make reasonable assessments of change-related factors, alone or with the help of others, and into the murky waters in which the organization operates. For example, if your change calls for hiring large numbers of technically skilled people, and these are not readily available in the labor market, perhaps you need to reconsider the change or what it will really take to make it happen (for example, shift work to another location, increase recruiting efforts, provide incentives, and so on). For those elements of the environment that are truly "murky," such as the outcome of an election, the move of a competitor, or the cost of gasoline, you can still engage in scenario planning in which you work through how your change will unfold or will need to be modified, under a number of different potential situations spanning from best to worst case.

Introducing efficiency-enhancing changes will be a lot easier when the external business environment is threatening. Introducing workplace modifications in a unionized setting is a lot easier when many jobs are being shipped offshore or plants are closing down. Introducing change when a major customer has defected may be a lot easier than if people perceive a "business as usual" condition.

WHAT DOES THE CHANGE LEADER DO WITH ALL THIS?

Given the multitude of considerations concerning WHAT, WHO, and CONTEXT, what is a change leader to do? First of all, having gone through this process, leaders are now faced with one of three choices (as per Figure 9.1):

- Go ahead and develop the change approach—the HOW.
- Use the situational assessment to revise the notion of WHAT needs changing, bringing it into closer alignment with the realities "on the ground" (that is, decide not to make the change, modify its nature or scope, or revise its timing).
- Identify one or more elements in the environment, critical to the target change, that will need to be modified before the desired change can be implemented.

Of course, we should again note that virtually all treatments of leadership presume a proactive leader. When it comes to change leadership, however, the decision to do nothing, hold off, do less, or do it more slowly is often the truly intelligent and courageous leadership decision. Putting all the pieces together is the best chance to reach that conclusion.

THE CHANGE PROCESS

For all three choices, the leader is eventually confronted with the "HOW should I proceed" question. As previously noted, the majority of other books, articles, and seminars on organizational change focus their attention on addressing HOW to implement change, that is, the change *process*. The recommended process "dos" and "don'ts" of change implementation are the result of many years of practitioner and research observations about things that tend, in general, to help or hinder change implementation. These recommendations have become more or less generic, and excellent summaries can be found elsewhere, so will not be repeated here.[3]

For example, we've all heard about the need for a change vision; the importance of communication; the need to motivate people to change by means of creating a "burning platform"; and the importance of involving others, celebrating victories, and reinforcing the appropriate behaviors. These recommendations are based on a great deal of evidence that if leaders do not effectively communicate, motivate, involve, or reinforce, the results of change efforts will often be disappointing. Surely, if leaders all followed these prescriptions, most changes would turn out well. But, they don't! Why?

Perhaps it is because they simply ignore these prescriptions, letting good changes falter for lack of good process. Maybe, as we noted earlier, leaders dutifully apply these prescriptions to the wrong changes, or at the wrong time, or in the wrong setting. How often have we seen full-blown "change programs," including extensive use of implementation teams; communication campaigns; HR and consultant involvement; and even T-shirts, coffee mugs, and fanciful names for the program (Top Gun, Project Phoenix, Campaign 2010, Way Forward), fail to deliver? This may be why, even with all that has been written about change management processes, even those who practice what is preached are often faced with disappointing outcomes.

It could be that other factors in the environment torpedoed the change and should have been tackled first. Perhaps change efforts fail because they take these prescriptions too literally, assuming they are universal when, in fact, they ultimately are situationally contingent (as our data and many of our examples have indicated). Thus there are many ways to fail in the change business, and faulty process is but one of them.

When the proper change strategizing has taken place, and it results in a decision to make a change, HOW to proceed *now* becomes the issue. That is why we've relegated this discussion of change process to the very end of the book. It is not possible to think about the process to be used *unless the process elements are linked to specific process concerns that have become apparent through diagnosis of WHAT, WHO, and CONTEXT.*

Do you want to create a heightened sense of urgency if people are already finding themselves unable to cope with the current turbulence? What are your communication challenges if your credibility with followers is low, or if the organizational culture is already highly cynical about most or all communications from its leaders? Should you involve or empower everyone to help with the change effort, or only some, and if so, who and when? In other words, the change process recommendations we've all seen or read about represent potential tools in your toolbox. They are good tools. But as with all tools, you need to have a sense of when to use them and how to use them depending on the problem and the entire situation at hand.

Thus leaders need to take the conventional process prescriptions and translate how each might apply in the particular situation. For example, if the context is highly turbulent to begin with, the organization is in decline, and everyone recognizes it, "creating a sense of urgency" may foster a sense of hopelessness or alarm that is counterproductive. Instead, bringing clarity and focus to a few key issues makes much more sense.

That is what Bethune did at Continental Airlines. While other airline executives were huddling with consultants conjuring up changes in operations, maintenance, pricing, financing, and marketing, and besieging their employees with dire talk about the industry, Bethune concluded that the only way people would fly Continental is if they got better service. The only way to do that was to reward employees for giving better service (a consideration of WHO), and to clearly communicate (a HOW issue) a simple WHAT. He told his employees that passengers "want to get to Atlanta safely, on time, and with their underwear."[4]

Conversely, a complacent culture riding on its past successes, but which may not be aware that it is out of step with future requirements, might require the establishment of a sense of urgency—but such would be difficult to achieve given the complacency. Instead of empowering followers to implement a change conceived by the leader, running the risk that they will stonewall it, the leader would be better off empowering followers to examine the business and the threats, and arrive at their own business case for making a change.

In the early 1990s, the CEO of Pepsi-Cola, Craig Weatherup, sensed decreased opportunities for maintaining the aggressive annual earnings increases the company had enjoyed. He felt something had to be done, and did his own investigation and analysis, but knew that the rest of his organization did not necessarily share his perceptions of the urgency to change. He took his direct reports on a retreat at which he first exhorted them with a vivid description, based on his analysis, of the organizational pain that was about to befall the company. He referred to it as his "freight train" speech. "There's a freight train out there, and it's called 15% earnings. We're standing on the track, and we'd better figure out something or it will run us right over."[5]

Although he probably had his own ideas about what needed changing, he did not put these out to the group. Instead, he had them brainstorm about what changes were likely to help achieve the earnings growth target. The group came up with many changes, discussed and consolidated them, and finally voted for the most promising ones, with the top five alternatives being chosen for further consideration. Managers were broken into five teams and asked to devote half their time for the following six weeks to investigate their assigned alternative.[6] These team assignments and discoveries then became the basis for directing future change initiatives and enlisting lower levels of the organization in the efforts.

The point of these examples is to alert the reader to the fact that process recommendations are rather generic and not situation- or setting-specific; as such, how to use them, when to use them, or in what combinations needs to be considered. There are times for lofty visions; there are times to focus on the here and now; there are times to broadly involve as many people as possible; there are times to involve just a few, or even none; there are times to set people's platforms on fire; there are times to calm the situation down in anticipation of the upcoming change.

The only more or less universal process recommendations involve the need to communicate whatever it is that we choose to do, reinforce people for behaving in ways that support the change, and remove obstacles in the path of the change. Even these steps, however, need to be tailored on the basis of a change situation assessment. Thus, beware of the "five," "six," or "seven easy steps" to change management.

CONCLUSION

In this chapter we tried to demonstrate that the change model, although complex, when broken down to its component parts can be used to diagnose a change situation. This process of taking one factor at a time should at least alert leaders to major issues they're likely to encounter, cause them to think about whether such issues can be appropriately addressed, and get them thinking about the processes they will use for everything from solution identification to implementation.

If the model leads you to conclude that your original WHAT may not be doable in its current form, that another change may be more suitable to the situation, or that something needs to be changed before proceeding with the target change, the model can again be used to analyze the revised change proposal. In the final chapter, we illustrate how all these factors within the model interact and how we need to manage the interplay between them.

10

SMART CHANGE LEADERS—

THEY GET IT!

"What's impressive is the speed with which he has galvanized an organization that was so depressed."

Wall Street analyst commenting on pharmaceutical firm Merck's recovery[1]

Quick—who's Richard Clark? Most people wouldn't recognize the name. He's the unassuming, unglamorous, nonboisterous CEO of Merck & Co. He assumed the post in 2005, at the low point in the company's 114-year history, facing a flood of lawsuits stemming from the failed drug Vioxx, the expiration of patents on other major money makers, and an R&D machine that seemed to have fizzled out. He has since engineered both a financial and credibility turnaround. Just like the often-heard lament that good kids don't get on the evening news, only the bad ones do, it seems that bad change leaders get lots of press while good ones often shun the limelight.

In this, our last chapter, we want to illustrate some examples of smart change leadership. The success of these leaders was not a function of following any one formula, prescription, or universal set of recommendations concerning how to implement change. The leaders in these examples did not follow the same recipe; they did not have one "silver bullet"; they did not tackle the same things in the same way.

We want to close by reinforcing the message, one more time, that smart change leadership is about recognizing, diagnosing, tailoring, balancing, and otherwise adapting one's hoped-for outcomes and implementation strategies to the realities of the situation. We believe that if any one of these leaders, or for that matter, other successful change leaders (whether mentioned in this book or not) were to have simply copied another change leader, followed a prescribed set of steps for change, or taken their guidance from parables or fables about change, they would have failed!

By necessity, the model presented in Chapter 2 was expanded in subsequent chapters *one element at a time* (leader, follower, context). In Chapter 9, we provided suggestions for critical questions leaders might ask as they're working their way through the various elements of the model. The reality is, however, that these elements are in constant interplay, interacting and affecting each other, thus affecting one's assessment of the overall situation. Change leaders do not have the luxury of taking them one at a time. Not only do the elements of our model interact, but they are also dynamic, changing as leaders are trying to incorporate them into their thinking. These dynamics need to be tracked and incorporated into one's thinking about further changes.

A good example of such dynamism might be the shift in the external environment recently experienced by Alan Mulally, the new CEO at Ford. Organized labor has always been seen as a major obstacle to any attempts to change the fortunes of a domestic car company. This view is based largely on the big-three car companies' past adversarial history with the unions. Shortly after Mulally took the job at Ford, Chrysler was sold to a private equity firm, which has already put union leaders on notice that drastic changes in work rules, benefits, and retiree health care costs will need to be made.

If they succeed in significantly altering the labor-management equation in the industry, Mulally would benefit from these changes, illustrating how changes in the external environment may alter one's thinking about what changes are realistically attainable. What seemed unchangeable before the Chrysler sale may now become worthy of consideration, or eventually even achievable.

Ultimately, the savvy change leader juggles all elements of the situation, engages in parallel rather than serial processing, and arrives at decisions about what to change and what implementation process to use; in part, this is why change leadership is so difficult. Thus the successful change leader assesses the business imperative and iteratively or simultaneously combines this evaluation with assessments of the consequences of choosing different change options given what is known about the leader, the followers, and the context.

In the following sections, we will highlight a few effective change leaders who apparently understand the complexity of change. The major point of these examples is that the search for the one "right" approach to change or the one "right" type of change leader is futile. The only thing these leaders have in common is that their behaviors were appropriate for the realities of the situation they were facing. What they all have in common is that they illustrate a change savvy of the type we've talked about throughout this book.

RICHARD CLARK AT MERCK & CO.

Change Situation

As we noted earlier, Richard Clark was brought in to resuscitate Merck & Co. after a series of events had left it reeling. Lawsuits, failed drugs, and a weak drug pipeline had tarnished its once solid reputation and led to a loss of support from the investment community. Clark was a thirty-five-year company veteran who had been promoted from nonglamorous manufacturing and thus had very low visibility on the outside, but did enjoy a good reputation on the inside, based mostly on his drives for greater efficiencies.

Though the company was blessed with a strong and loyal workforce, morale was down due to the constant struggles with legal and business problems. Progress in new drug development was hobbled by a structure and a bureaucratic culture that slowed the drug-development process, and a reward system that promoted risk-avoidance and a reluctance to terminate lagging projects. Along with other large pharmaceutical firms, Merck was experiencing increased competition from generics and from smaller biotech firms, coupled with pressures from the insurance industry to contain the cost of prescription drugs.

Leader's Response

Clark now admits that he had "no clue" as to a turnaround plan when he first became CEO.[2] He combined his assessment of the business imperatives with his deep knowledge of the company to conclude that what needed changing was the whole way the organization looked at drug development. Specifically, he focused on removing barriers to such development that had been built over time. He understood that to get at the underlying problems, he'd have to offer more than a typical reorganization and layoffs that are such common responses to adversity (though one of his earliest changes was a cost-cutting program).

With revamping the drug-development process becoming his WHAT, he launched several major subchanges in the hopes of getting there. He tackled the structural impediments by creating teams around therapeutic agendas such as diabetes, often taking the members out of their functional silos so that scientists, marketers, and manufacturing types were on the same team. To better focus the development process as well as speed it up, he pushed these teams to improve their interaction with the external environment, namely physicians, patients, and the insurance companies.

The improved coordination and early warnings about issues that might affect one or more constituencies created some early successes, as drugs were better focused on potential demand. Moreover, promising drugs moved through the Merck pipeline faster, got quicker FDA approval, came to market faster, and had greater support from insurance companies. These successes motivated employees to embrace the approach and push even harder to help with the turnaround, and made them more receptive to further changes.

In examining its portfolio of drug-development projects, Merck noticed a reluctance to terminate projects with poor prospects, thus preventing the shifting of resources to more promising ones. The company began offering stock options to scientists who terminated their own lagging projects. This was aimed at rewarding people for being realistic and accepting failure as part of any discovery process. It encouraged them to move on. All models of innovation talk of the need to accept and not punish failure. Merck changed its reward system as a means of trying to move in the direction of such a cultural change.

Although it's too early to judge the ultimate success of Clark's tenure, this example illustrates how changes in the drug-development process were implemented in a setting-specific way that consisted of multiple changes. Furthermore, each of these, and the processes used to implement them, were more or less attuned to the realities of the organization; its external environment; and the skills, resources, and culture of the company, as well as being a capitalization on who the change leader was and what he brought to the table.

Clark used every element of our change model. He started out with an ambitious WHAT, change the drug-development process. However, to get there, the initial changes were very focused. He did not start by making wholesale changes affecting everything all at once, as other leaders we have discussed tended to do. This could have thrown the entire organization into chaos. He realized from his assessment of WHO and CONTEXT that to get there he would need several subchanges. He made structural changes, reward system changes, and teamwork changes, and changed the way the company engaged its external environment. He did all this by leveraging his own "buckets" of influence, while engaging and fully utilizing his followers' capabilities. In the process, he increased his credibility and capacity for further change.

It is worth noting that Clark's approach in creating cross-functional, therapy-focused teams was not all that different from the earlier discussed CDC director's change for addressing public health problems. What was different was that Merck faced a widely perceived crisis, whereas the CDC did not; Clark possessed personal credibility and a deep knowledge of the company and its culture, which Julie Gerberding did not; and the pressures (internal and external) in a publicly held company are quite different from those in a government agency (not to mention differences in career orientations, incentives, job security provisions, and so on). The WHAT may have been similar, but the WHO and the CONTEXT clearly were not.

A. G. LAFLEY AT PROCTER & GAMBLE

Change Situation

A. G. Lafley was named to replace Durk Jager and restore calm after Jager's tumultuous and short reign at Procter & Gamble (P&G). He understood that Jager had tried to implement too many changes too quickly, even if some of them were, in the long run, necessary (Jacques Nasser's problem at Ford). Interestingly, however, since his arrival, Lafley has transformed P&G way beyond what people had expected of him. How did he do it? He did it largely through a difference in style, or change savvy. "Where Jager was gruff, Lafley is soothing. Where Jager bullied, Lafley persuades. He listens more than he talks. He is living proof that the messenger is just as important as the message." As one division president said, "People want to follow him." Another associate noted, "People wanted him to succeed."[3]

The culture at P&G was stodgy and inbred. Long-term managers, promoted from within, were highly resistant to change. Unlike in the situation at Merck, many leaders and others were largely in denial, having great faith in the strengths and ultimate success of their brands. Yet increased competition from other companies, the need to do better in foreign markets, and increased demands for lower prices and conformity to large customers' business models were taking their toll.

Lafley was a company man who joined at age twenty-nine as a brand assistant. He gained the attention of senior leaders and climbed to be head of P&G's soap and detergent business, headed the Asian division, and then ran the entire North American operations. His reputational "bucket" was full. In addition, he was known as a good mentor and for developing his staff by giving them broad responsibilities. He is known to be humble rather than flamboyant; possesses a soothing, soft-spoken, and persuasive style; is a good listener; and, while not charismatic, is certainly charming. He recognized that people and brands were the company's major assets, but also that the previous CEO's mismanaged change initiatives had left many feeling beleaguered and wondering about the company's direction.

Leader's Response

Lafley responded at two levels. At one level he had a deeply held belief, similar to his activist predecessor, that the company needed to change in the most fundamental ways. However, he did not make grand pronouncements, or articulate a grandiose vision; if he had one, he was keeping it to himself. Instead, he embarked on a series of targeted changes that, before one knew it, constituted a meaningful transformation. He first enacted what seemed like much smaller, less threatening, and clearly welcomed changes, while constantly chipping away at people's views of what was necessary, communicating nonstop about how and why the company needed to change.

He started out by appealing to his managers' strengths and biases. He told them, "Focus on what you do well—selling the company's major brands . . . instead of trying to develop the next big thing."[4] Although this was clearly aimed at reassuring the troops, it also motivated them to do what they knew how, and paved the way for the acceptance of other changes that were more revolutionary for the company, such as outsourcing certain functions and growing by acquisition rather than only through innovation from within.

At the same time, Lafley communicated through strong symbolic actions. He stripped away many of the trappings of power at the executive level, moved division presidents to the same floor as their staffs, broke down walls and replaced them with open offices, and replaced a rectangular conference table with a round one, where he listens more often than he talks, coaching others as they share ideas.

This "charm offensive," as some have called it, has allowed him to create changes that smoothed the way for future changes, such as the eventual replacement of many top executives, and to increase the diversity of the senior leadership team. These alterations, in turn, paved the way for some of his major changes, such as making major acquisitions, proclaiming that in the future one-half of P&G's products should come from the outside, and outsourcing some manufacturing and IT. These significant departures from P&G's previous business model might not have gone as well had they not been built on the foundation of the other changes.

Thus Lafley has accomplished a remarkable transformation, yet he never called it such; he drove major change, but he broke it down to component changes and carefully strategized and nurtured each, being patient to see the results. He was alert to the limits of executive power, realizing that his people and his brands were all he had and that these would have to be at the core of his changes.

He showed a deep understanding of the change dilemma, noting that "I am worried that I will ask the organization to change ahead of its understanding, capability, and commitment."[5] He says that he learned from the failure of his predecessor. "I avoided saying P&G people were bad, I enrolled them in change." In fact, he realized that the culture, though "insular" in some ways, also represented a major strength that could help him if he could harness it. He reinforced the deeply held values and beliefs of employees, thus better enabling him to challenge some of the more peripheral ones that needed changing.

Like Clark at Merck, Lafley first seemed the antithesis of the change leader some companies think they need. Yet his understanding of the business imperative, assessment of the situation, and personal attributes combined to create successful change. Like Clark, he broke his grand plan into a series of smaller changes (WHAT). He made changes in personnel yet took advantage of the people there and understood his own sources of influence (WHO). He took account of and tried to modify the culture, yet appealed to its strengths (CONTEXT).

ALAN MULALLY AT FORD

Change Situation

The situation at Ford is dire, and Alan Mulally was recruited from Boeing to try to turn around this troubled company. As of this writing, it's way too early to predict what Mulally's tenure will be known for. We have no idea if he will succeed or not. However, we want to use him as an illustration of savvy change leadership, early on in the change process, on the part of an outsider coming into an extremely challenging situation. We want to focus on how he is laying the groundwork for whatever changes he has in mind, or even how he plans to arrive at change ideas. This is really about how he is *proceeding* rather than any particular changes he is currently making.

The dynamics of the automobile industry and Ford's precarious situation are so well-known that we will go directly to a discussion of how this outsider seems to be approaching the task of changing the company. The specific nature of upcoming changes has, by and large, not even crystallized, as he focuses on his diagnosis and situational assessment. Up to now, most of his changes are of the "collateral" type; that is, he is changing the situation so as to enable the main change goal, which has to be to rebuild a dysfunctional culture and efficiently produce cars that people want to buy.

As a leader, Mulally brings with him the disadvantage of the outsider to both the company and the industry. However, having led a successful turnaround at Boeing, he does have some reputational credits in his bucket. Facing the challenges of an industry in trouble, the lack of industry experience, a company in a tailspin, and shell-shocked employees, and having replaced a member of the Ford family as CEO, how has he been tackling his job?

Leader's Response

From early observations and reports, he is doing a variety of things right. We noted earlier the oft-heard recommendation to "create a sense of urgency" as the first step in creating change. We also commented that this may be dysfunctional in a setting in which people are already stressed out by conditions widely known to all. In fact, Mulally reportedly is going around Detroit telling his audiences of employees and dealers that "It's going to be OK,"[6] and as if to reassure them, he reminds them that Boeing is okay even though things looked pretty bleak after the September 11 terror attacks. He is trying to calm things down instead of whipping them up!

In an interview with the *Wall Street Journal*,[7] he made the following observations about the process he is using to change the company, or more accurately, to prepare it to change. First he says, upon arriving at Ford, "I listened to everybody. . . . You talk to all the stakeholders. . . . You talk to customers, dealers, Ford employees, UAW, your suppliers, your investors, everybody." He then goes on to say that all this has provided excellent feedback about what's going on, and that feedback is useful for developing a strategy and a plan for *dealing with reality.* This is a good example of what we earlier said differentiates business strategy done in the abstract, or textbook fashion, from change strategizing, namely, adapting the WHAT you would like to accomplish to the situation at hand.

Not only is he reserving his plan until he's done a lot of listening (by now a recurring theme among our more savvy change leaders, though often seen as a weakness on the part of Wall Street and the business press), he also has resisted the temptation to churn a lot of the senior leadership. Although in this situation it wouldn't be surprising if he did so, since these are the people that didn't get the job done previously, Mulally says he has "elevated people to the table, to the team, that need to be there." By perusing personnel records he had a great deal of information about each senior leader, but what he needed to see was how they worked together and acted when they were at the table. Again, many outsiders feel more comfortable bringing in their own people—Mullaly played the cards he was dealt, but has been watching and assessing them carefully.

Finally, we see that Mulally understands that cultural change is essential for any long-term changes at the company. Yet, unlike Clark at Merck or Lafley at P&G, he approaches such change judiciously in recognition of his status as the new kid on the block. By encouraging others to do as much fact finding as he's doing, he is promoting self-discovery and identification of problems, rather than being the one who "tells" others what the problems are.

A wonderful illustration of his push toward self-discovery was his taking two senior engineers on a trip to *Consumer Report*'s car-testing facility for a briefing on what the testers thought about the current lineup of Ford vehicles. Known for their impartial and often brutal assessment of products, the testers gave hours of examples of disappointing engineering on Ford cars. When the engineers began to get defensive and tried to explain their choices, Mulally stepped in, handed each a pad, and said "You know what? Let's just listen and take notes."[8] Nor did he restrict this type of factfinding to his reports. Mulally himself role modeled this behavior when he went on a personal pilgrimage to Toyota. Although in Detroit it may raise eyebrows when an automobile company CEO visits "the enemy," he was not abashed to admit that he admired Toyota and hoped to learn from them.

He understood that no matter how much the culture needs changing from one that is smug and defensive, and that explains away problems rather than owning and fixing them, his saying so as an outsider would not do it. Hearing it from influential industry players was far more effective. He is teaching people that outsiders are the enemy only in an insular culture. These outsiders may hold key information needed to make fundamental changes in the company. In this and similar ways he is chipping away at cultural impediments to larger changes at the company.

Will he succeed? Who knows? However, given his understanding of what he brings to the table as a leader, his ongoing assessment of his followers, and his growing appreciation of the internal and external environment through his extensive talking and listening, he seems to have a better shot than most outsiders who come with a heavy dose of arrogance and pronounce themselves to be just what the doctor ordered.

In terms of our model, Mulally is actually holding off on the WHAT, choosing instead to have a good grasp of WHO and CONTEXT. Under WHO, he is cognizant of his own strengths and weaknesses in the leadership position. But he is also weighing the trade-offs between replacing key executives and tapping their experience by better involving them in the rebuilding, thereby also getting to know them better. Under CONTEXT, he senses what needs to change internally, but he is trying to make such changes by increasing interactions with external constituencies, much like Clark has done with insurance companies and physicians. However, those changes that did not require the active support of employees, like putting some of the car brands owned by Ford up for sale, he undertook more or less immediately. Conceivably, Ford employees might be pleased that the money raised by such sales may increase the resources available to fix some of their problems.

CONCLUSION

Change can be effectively led. Smart change leaders size up what they want to accomplish and then take stock of what they have to work with: who they are, who they are leading, and what the various internal and external influences are that need to be considered. Thus they arrive at a change strategy that shapes their idea for the nature of the change and lays out the details of how to go about it.

Lafley, as a respected, accomplished, well-liked insider, can probe, coach, and nudge people to go along with his changes using positional, reputational, and personal influence strategies. Mulally can't do that. He needs an approach that allows others to arrive at the answers without him "telling" them. However, Mulally, and for that matter Clark, probably have more motivated audiences than Lafley to the degree that Ford and Merck people are (were) more alarmed at their predicaments than were those at P&G. Clark had both a crisis and the insider status going for him, but he also correctly translated the business imperative into a series of changes for the drug-development process that were, in combination, responsive to the strategic demands of the situation. Mulally is not rushing into his WHATs, seemingly waiting until he's finished assessing the situation.

As we bring this book to a close, we want to leave the reader with the following thoughts. It is not simply the industry leaders find themselves in, nor the type of change they're facing, nor the type of leader they are, nor the types of people they're asking to embrace the change, nor the situation surrounding the change that singly determines their approach to making meaningful organizational changes—it's all of these things. Smart change leaders understand this complexity and act accordingly. If we examine changes that have not worked out well, we will usually find (barring unforeseen events) that the change leaders failed to take this more difficult, yet productive road.

We hope that we have challenged much of the conventional wisdom about change and replaced it with new and richer insights. Leading change is not about following a set pattern of steps, it's about leadership in the broader sense of the word, and it's about relationships. Only when those relationships are not yet formed do prescriptive "dos" and "don'ts" play a role. Change is not only about the leader and what he or she does, as has often been suggested. It's about the task at hand, the followers needed to implement it, and the environment in which it is to take place. Change is not just about proclaiming visions; it is as much or more about listening, analyzing, seeking to understand, and then acting. "Change or perish" may be the kiss of death if it's used as an excuse for a frantic proactivity that lacks the foundation of analysis and discernment.

People do not "naturally" resist change; they resist change they do not understand, the value of which they do not see, or the demands of which they cannot meet. It is a change leader's job to motivate others to follow and to make it possible for them to do so. Change leaders are not born. They come in all shapes and sizes, but they work with what they have, and can achieve success using many approaches, as long as what they do fits with the situation in which they find themselves. People are not unfortunate obstacles to change plans; they are the key elements in these plans. Cultivating people's commitment to the organization and to the leader may be the most important change tool leaders have.

Finally, encouraging people to think about "managing change," as a singular, episodic event, the way it is portrayed in most books and articles, may be a major disservice to leaders everywhere. How any one change turns out is a function of changes past, changes present, and the other influences discussed throughout this book. Previous change episodes will have shaped beliefs about the current change; these same events will have also affected the leader-follower relationship; the nature of these beliefs and relationships will affect people's motivation and commitment to implement the change; and the latter will be affected by the turbulence of the current change environment.

Shortcuts around these realities are paths to failure for the organization, the leader, or both. You cannot just copy what someone or some other organization has done and expect it to work. Nor can you buy "off the shelf" answers, regardless of how obviously good the solution appears to be. Leading meaningful and lasting change requires juggling many competing interests, understanding the full situation, and then often making some tough decisions. The concepts and examples we've covered were meant to provide a realistic guide for this difficult process. Being able to successfully lead change in organizations may be the most important skill required of today's leaders. We hope this book will serve as a valuable reference by providing effective ways to think through upcoming change situations and thus help all of us improve our change "batting average," perhaps even getting us voted into the change hall of fame.

REFERENCE MATTER

NOTES

PREFACE

1. Lavelle, L. In brief. *BusinessWeek,* February 28, 2005 (online).
2. Why the boss really had to say goodbye. *BusinessWeek,* July 4, 2005 (online).
3. Tale of two CEOs: How public perception shapes reputations. *Wall Street Journal,* July 12, 2006, p. A2.

CHAPTER 1

1. The 9/11 report. *New York Times,* July 23, 2004, p. 1.
2. Organizing for successful change management. *McKinsey Quarterly,* July 2006.
3. Our challenge is change, not globalization. *Forbes,* November 27, 2006 (online).
4. CEOs find innovation hard to achieve. *Reuters.com,* March 1, 2006.
5. Wetlaufer, S. The business case against revolution. *Harvard Business Review,* February 2001, pp. 113–119.
6. How a highflier in marketing fell at Wal-Mart. *Wall Street Journal,* December 11, 2006, pp. A1, A16.
7. Five years of change. *Atlanta Journal and Constitution,* January 1, 2006, pp. F1, F5.
8. A digital evolution at Kodak. *New York Times,* January 7, 2006, Sec. 3, p. 3.
9. Ford: Why it's worse than you think. *BusinessWeek,* June 25, 2001 (online).
10. Ibid.
11. P&G: New and improved. *BusinessWeek,* July 7, 2003 (online).

CHAPTER 3

1. When organization is not enough. *McKinsey Quarterly,* March 2006.
2. Less may be more at Microsoft. *BusinessWeek,* October 3, 2005 (online).

3. Remaking Microsoft. *BusinessWeek,* May 17, 1999 (online).

4. Cascio, W. F. Strategies for responsible restructuring. *Academy of Management Executive,* 2002, *16,* 80–91.

5. Uchitelle, L. *The Disposable American.* New York: Vintage Books, 2007.

6. Up front. *BusinessWeek,* November 6, 2006 (online).

7. The mouse that roared. *Fortune,* July 23, 2007, pp. 84–88.

8. Liu, Y., Fedor, D. B., Herold, D. M., and Caldwell, S. D. The impact of conscientiousness, change support and change attribution on change fairness perceptions: A multi-level investigation. Paper presented at the Southern Management Association meeting, Clearwater, Florida, October 2006.

CHAPTER 4

1. Lessons from Larry. *BusinessWeek,* March 6, 2006 (online).

2. Fiorina had a vision for HP, and some credit for its turnaround. *New York Times,* October 6, 2006, p. C-3; Tossing out a chief executive. *New York Times,* February 14, 2005, p. C-1.

3. Herold, D. M., Fedor, D. B., Caldwell, S. D., and Liu, Y. The effects of transformational leadership and change leadership on employees' commitment to a change: A multi-level study. *Journal of Applied Psychology,* 2008.

CHAPTER 5

1. Chanel's American in Paris. *BusinessWeek,* January 29, 2007 (online).

2. Being mean is so last millennium. *BusinessWeek,* January 15, 2007 (online).

3. Nissan's boss, *BusinessWeek,* October 4, 2004.

4. Xerox: The downfall. *BusinessWeek,* March 5, 2001 (online).

5. Ibid.

6. Renovating Home Depot. *BusinessWeek,* March 6, 2006 (online).

7. Back from the brink. *Wall Street Journal,* April 24, 2006, pp. B1, B3.

8. In this corner: The contender. *Fortune,* April 3, 2006 (online).

9. P&G: New and improved. *BusinessWeek,* July 7, 2003 (online).

10. The outsider, *Fortune,* October 16, 2006 (online).

11. Pfeffer, J., and Sutton, R. I. *Hard facts, dangerous half-truths and total nonsense.* Boston: Harvard Business School Press, 2006.

CHAPTER 6

1. Why is this man smiling? *Fortune,* October 18, 2004, pp. 130–138.

2. Congress looks at allegations of discord at CDC, *Atlanta Journal and Constitution,* May 24, 2006, pp. A1, A15.

3. Exodus, morale shake CDC. *Atlanta Journal and Constitution,* September 10, 2006, pp. A1, A15.

4. E-mail from CDC director to CDC employees dated September 22, 2006.

5. Here we are only addressing cognitive motivational processes. Psychologists also recognize that noncognitive, subconscious, or unconscious motivational forces affect human behavior.

6. Caldwell, S. D., Herold, D. M., and Fedor, D. B. Toward an understanding of the relationship between organizational change, individual differences, and changes in person-environmental fit: A cross-level study. *Journal of Applied Psychology*, 2004, *89*, 868–882.

7. Herold, D. M., Davis, W., Fedor, D. B., and Parsons, C. Dispositional influences on transfer of learning in multi-stage training programs. *Personnel Psychology*, 2002, *55*, 851–869.

8. Herold, D. M., Fedor, D. F., and Caldwell, S. D. Beyond change management: A multilevel investigation of contextual and personal influences on employees' commitment to change. *Journal of Applied Psychology*, 2007, *92*, 942–951.

9. Herold, D. M., Fedor, D. B., Caldwell, S. D., and Liu, Y. The effects of transformational leadership and change leadership on employees' commitment to a change: A multi-level study. *Journal of Applied Psychology*, 2008.

10. The professional organizer. *BusinessWeek*, September 3, 2007 (online).

11. Turning shopping trips into treasure hunts. *Wall Street Journal*, August 27, 2007, pp. B1, B3.

CHAPTER 7

1. The truth about Tiger, *Golf Digest*, January 2005 (online).

2. Fedor, D. B., and Rowland, K. M. Supervisor attributions for subordinate performance. *Journal of Management*, 1989, *15*, 37–48.

CHAPTER 8

1. My year at Wal-Mart. *BusinessWeek*, February 12, 2007 (online).

2. Translating the Toyota Way. *New York Times*, February 15, 2007, p. C1.

3. Ibid.

4. Malone, M. S. *Bill & Dave: How Hewlett and Packard built the world's greatest company.* New York: Penguin Group, 2007.

5. My year at Wal-Mart, *BusinessWeek*, February 12, 2007 (online).

6. Banker to the rich, U.S. Trust stumbles after sale to Schwab. *Wall Street Journal*, September 15, 2004, pp. A1, A6.

7. Herold, D. M., Fedor, D. F., and Caldwell, S. D. Beyond change management: A multilevel investigation of contextual and personal influences on employees' commitment to change. *Journal of Applied Psychology*, 2007, *92*, 942–951.

CHAPTER 9

1. Duck, D. J. Managing change: The art of balancing. *Harvard Business Review*, November–December, 1993, pp. 1–10.

2. At 3M, a struggle between efficiency and creativity. *BusinessWeek,* June 11, 2007 (online).

3. Kotter, J. P. *Leading change.* Boston: Harvard Business School Press, 1996; Beer, M., Eisenstat, A., and Spector, B. Why change programs don't produce change. *Harvard Business Review,* November-December 1990, pp. 158–166.

4. Why is this man smiling? *Fortune,* October 18, 2004, pp. 130–138.

5. Times are good? Create a crisis. *Fortune,* June 28, 1993, pp. 123–130.

6. Garvin, D., and Sull, D. Pepsi's regeneration, 1990–1993. Harvard Business School Case.

CHAPTER 10

1. Is Merck's medicine working? *BusinessWeek,* July 30, 2007 (online).

2. Ibid.

3. P&G: How A. G. Lafley is revolutionizing a bastion of corporate conservatism. *BusinessWeek,* July 7, 2003 (online).

4. Ibid.

5. Ibid.

6. At Ford, the "outsider" is optimistic. *Wall Street Journal,* July 23, 2007.

7. Ibid.

8. The new heat on Ford. *BusinessWeek,* June 4, 2007 (online).

INDEX

Failed outcomes
Summers, Larry, 43
Support resources, 102, 106, 121, 122, 124
Sutton, R. I., 69
SWAT teams, 96–97
Synergies, 32, 36, 38

Team-based initiatives, 86, 96–97, 128, 133
Technological changes, 4, 13, 88–89, 97
Technology environment, 10, 31, 103, 113
Telecommuting, 102
Thoman, Richard, 2, 60–61, 65, 120
3M Corporation, 118–119
360 feedback, 53
Time-Warner, 32
Timelines, 98, 99, 110
Tindell, Kip, 82
Toyota, 96–97, 101, 103, 139
Tracking changes, 13, 33, 55, 91, 97–99, 110, 131
Training, 85–86, 90, 96, 97, 98, 105–106
Transformational leadership, 51–52
Triage, 42
Trotman, Alex, 12
Troubleshooting, 96–97
Turnover of employees, 4, 37, 46, 63, 100, 107, 123–124
2006 elections, 2

Uchitelle, Louis, 30
University of Colorado, 30
Unrealistic expectations, 5, 37, 87, 89–92, 97

Unsatisfactory outcomes. *See* Failed outcomes
Urgency, sense of, 2–5, 51, 53, 58–59, 63, 71, 127–128, 137–138
U.S. Trust, 107

Vendors, 11, 19, 42, 46, 92, 97, 101–102, 124
Vioxx, 130
Vision, xi-xii, 16, 51, 53, 114, 126, 128
Volkswagen, 32

Wall Street, xi, 10, 11, 64, 130, 138
Wall Street Journal, 138
Wal-Mart, 7, 100, 107
War room, 110
Weatherup, Craig, 128
Welch, Jack, xiv
WHAT factors, 18–24, 27, 29–42, 62, 92, 96, 114, 125–127
WHO factors, 19–24, 27, 40, 96, 114, 116, 125–127
Who Moved My Cheese (Johnson), x, 72
Woertz, Patricia, 68, 69
Woods, Tiger, 85, 91–92
Work redistribution. *See* Restructuring
Workforce. *See* Employees; Followers
Work-life balances, 9, 36

Xerox, 2, 9, 60–61, 63–65, 81, 120

Zaleznik, Abraham, 43